The State
of
Church Giving
through 1994

John L. Ronsvalle

Sylvia Ronsvalle

empty tomb, inc.

Champaign, Illinois

The State of Church Giving through 1994 by John and Sylvia Ronsvalle
published by empty tomb, inc.
First printing, December 1996

empty tomb, inc.
301 North Fourth Street
P.O. Box 2404
Champaign, Illinois 61825-2404
Phone: (217) 356-9519
Fax: (217) 356-2344

ISBN 0-9639962-5-8

Contents

98042

Tables and Figures

Preface

Each year as this annual update is prepared, the valuable nature of the historical record presented in the *Yearbook of American and Canadian Churches* series, and its predecessor publications, becomes apparent once again. The National Council of the Churches of Christ in the U.S.A. has continued to publish the data, making it available to scholars and other interested people. Joan B. Campbell, General Secretary, and the Office of Communication, should be acknowledged for the role this organization has played in making this information available in a usable format to the general public.

For the last several years, Kenneth B. Bedell, serving as the editor of the *Yearbook of American and Canadian Churches*, has continued the tradition of the *Yearbook* and his work is also gratefully acknowledged.

The *YACC* series is built as well on the commitment of denominational officials who collect these statistics from their constituent congregations, and then forward them to the *YACC* office. Their efforts are an important factor in being able to understand church member giving patterns over a multiyear period.

We are always grateful for the general support we receive from the other empty tomb staff. In particular, David Cavanaugh and Sarah Hartmann assisted us in the production of this edition.

While many people contribute to an effort such as this, the authors, of course, take full responsibility for the content on the following pages. This report is offered in the hopes that it will contribute to a constructive dialogue that will assist the church in the United States in understanding its potential for sharing God's concern for a hurting world.

John L. Ronsvalle, Ph.D.
Sylvia Ronsvalle

Champaign, Illinois
December 1996

Summary

The State of Church Giving through 1994 is the most recent report in a series that considers denominational giving data for a set of denominations first included in a study published in 1988. The present report reviews data for 29 denominations, that include about 100,000 of the estimated 350,000 religious congregations in the U.S, and 30 million full or confirmed members.

The findings of the present church member giving analysis include:

- Giving as a percentage of income to Total Contributions decreased from the 1993 level. This was the ninth year in a row that this category experienced a decrease. Congregational Finances continued a pattern of alternately increasing and decreasing, with a decrease from 1993 to 1994. Giving to Benevolences as a percentage of income continued a decline for the ninth year in a row, the longest decline in the 1968-1994 period under review.

- When the composite group of 29 denominations was expanded to include 47 Protestant communions, similar patterns in giving were observed.

- An analysis of data for a subset of mainline Protestant denominations and a subset of evangelical Protestant denominations found giving higher in the evangelical Protestant denominations, but a steeper decline in giving patterns among the evangelicals.

- A review of giving patterns in 11 Protestant denominations from 1921 to 1994 found per member giving in constant 1987 dollars increased at the highest rate from 1947 to 1960. The average annual increase in per member giving to churches was $8.62 during this period, when U.S. per capita disposable personal income was increasing $113 a year in constant 1987 dollars. From 1950 to 1994, the period of highest annual increase in per member giving occurred from 1950 to 1955 in constant dollars, although the highest portion of annual per capita income increase donated was from 1955 to 1960. The period from 1960 to 1975 displayed an extended period of lower increases. The period 1980-1985 saw the highest annual average increase in per member giving since 1975.

- The continued decrease in per member giving to Benevolences as a percentage of income suggested that by the year A.D. 2048, 0% of income would be going beyond the congregation to Benevolences. The data pointed to the year A.D. 2199 for Congregational Finances reaching 0% of income.

• Declines in membership indicate that the historically Christian church, as defined by a combination of mainline Protestant, evangelical and conservative Protestant and the Roman Catholic Church, is being marginalized as a social institution in American society.

In addition, the last chapter in this edition provides summaries of special focus chapters which appeared in previous editions of *The State of Church Giving* series. These summaries include:

• A model of Catholic giving patterns

• A review of the Unified Theory of Giving and Membership;

• A review of a comparison of denominational reports with two other sources of charitable giving estimates;

• A consideration of consumer spending patterns in light of church giving data;

• A review of church member giving in first-year recession years;

• A comparison of the U.S. Social Health Index with per member giving to Benevolences as a percentage of income.

This chapter concludes with a discussion of approaches to research which were included in a panel presentation at the joint Religious Research Association and Society for the Scientific Study of Religion annual meeting in November 1996.

Introduction _____

On the following pages is an analysis of data which has been provided by approximately 100,000 congregations operating throughout the United States to their related denominations. Given that there are an estimated 350,000 religious congregations of any type in the U.S., the following aggregated information provides an important indication of how church members value their religious affiliation, as evidenced in giving patterns. The data was obtained as a consequence of a request by a relevant national or regional office which asked each congregation to provide membership data, as well as financial data. The data provides information about the operation of the congregation, termed Congregational Finances for purposes of this analysis, as well as activities that serve the larger mission of the church, labeled Benevolences. (For more detailed definitions of these categories, see the "Definition of Terms" section below.)

The denominational offices then compiled the data and published it in annual reports. The *Yearbook of American and Canadian Churches* (*YACC*), of the National Council of the Churches of Christ in the U.S.A., requested and compiled this data from the national denominational offices, publishing it in its annual editions.

The data published by the *YACC*, in some cases being combined with data obtained directly from a denominational source (as noted in Appendix B), serves as the basis for the present report.

A comparison of data for a given set of denominations over a period of years permits a review of patterns in giving. This denominational giving composite may also be used to compare subsets of denominations based, for example, on theological perspectives as self-identified by affiliation with national organizations.

Definition of Terms. The analyses in this report use certain terms which can be defined as follows.

In the various analyses, when the term "per member" is used, it refers to Full or Confirmed Members, unless otherwise noted. Full or Confirmed Members is consistently reported by the denominations in the present analysis. Certain denominations also report a larger figure for Inclusive Membership, which may include, for example, children who have been baptized but are not yet eligible for confirmation in that denomination. The category of Full or Confirmed Members is used in the present analysis because it is a relatively consistent category among the reporting denominations.

Total Contributions Per Member refers to the average contribution in either dollars or as a percentage of income which is donated to the denominations' affiliated congregations by Full or Confirmed Members in a given year.

Total Contributions combines two subcategories. The definitions used in this report for the two subcategories are consistent with the standardized *YACC* data request questionnaire.

The first subcategory is Congregational Finances, which includes all income directed to the internal operation of the individual congregation, including such items as the utility bills and salaries for the pastor and office staff, as well as Sunday school materials and capital programs.

The other subcategory is Benevolences. This category includes the congregation's external expenditures, beyond its own operations, for what might be termed the larger mission of the church. Benevolences includes international missions as well as national and local charities, through denominational channels as well as programs of nondenominational organizations to which the congregation contributes directly. Benevolences also includes support of denomination administration at all levels, donations to denominational seminaries and schools, and in at least one case, it includes pastor pension and medical support.

When the terms "income," "per capita income," and "giving as a percentage of income" are used, they refer to the U.S. Department of Commerce Bureau of Economic Analysis' U.S. Per Capita Disposable (after-tax) Personal Income series, unless otherwise noted.

The Implicit Price Deflator for National Income was used to convert current dollars to constant dollars, thus factoring out inflation and allowing dollar amounts to be compared among different years, unless otherwise specified.

Appendix C includes both U.S. Per Capita Disposable Personal Income figures and the Implicit Price Deflator for National Income figures used in this study.

Rounding Calculations. In most cases, Total Contributions, Total Congregational Contributions and Total Benevolences for the denominations being considered were divided by Full or Confirmed Membership in order to obtain per capita, or per member, data for that set of denominations. This procedure occasionally led to a small rounding discrepancy in one of the three related figures. That is, by a small margin, rounded per capita Total Contributions did not equal per capita Congregational Finances plus per capita Benevolences. Similarly, rounding data to the nearest dollar for use in tables and graphics led on occasion to a small rounding error in the data presented in tabular or graphic form.

Giving in Dollars. Per member giving to churches can be measured in dollars. The dollar measure indicates, among other information, how much money religious institutions have to spend. Did congregations have as much to spend in 1994 as they did in 1968? This question can be considered in both current dollars and constant dollars.

Current dollars indicate the value of the dollar in the year it was donated. However, since inflation changes the value of the dollar, data provided in current dollars has limited information value over a time span. If someone donated $5 in 1968 and $5 in 1994, on one level that person is donating the same amount of money. On another level, however, the buying power of that $5 has changed a great deal. Since less can be bought with the $5 donated in 1994 because of inflation in the economy, on a practical level the value of the donation has shrunk.

To account for the changes caused by inflation in the value of the dollar, a deflator can be applied. The result is constant dollars. Dollars adjusted to their constant dollar value through the use of a deflator can be more fairly compared over a time span since the dollars from different years have all been adjusted to have the value of one particular year.

The deflator most commonly applied in this analysis designated the base period as 1987, with levels in 1987 set equal to 100. Thus, when adjusted by the deflator, the 1968 gift of $5 was worth $15.97 in constant 1987 dollars, and the 1994 gift of $5 was worth $3.93 in constant 1987 dollars. Constant dollars provides a more realistic view of the value of church member gifts across various years than the current dollar value.

Giving as a Percentage of Income. There is another way to look at church member giving. This category is giving as a percentage of income. Considering what percentage or portion of income is donated to the religious congregation provides a different perspective. Rather than indicating how much money the congregation has to spend, as when one considers dollars donated, giving as a percentage of income indicates how the congregation rates in light of church members' total available incomes. Has the church sustained the same level of support from its members in comparison to previous years, as measured by what portion of income is being donated by members from the total resources available to them?

Percentage of income is a valuable measure because incomes change. Just as inflation changes the value of the dollar, so that $5 in 1968 is not the same as $5 in 1994, incomes, influenced by inflation and real growth, also change. If per capita income in 1968 was $3,077 in current dollars, and a church member gave $308 that year, that member would have been tithing, or giving the standard of ten percent. In contrast, if 1994 per capita income had increased to $19,253 in current dollars, and that church member still gave $308, the member would have been giving only 1.6% of income. The church would have commanded a smaller portion of the member's overall financial activity.

Thus, while dollars donated indicate how much the church has to spend, giving as a percentage of income provides some measure of the level of commitment the church member displays for the church in comparison to the church member's total spending. One might say that giving as a percentage of income is an indication of the church's "market share" of church members' lives.

In most cases, to obtain giving as a percentage of income, total income to a set of denominations was divided by the number of Full or Confirmed Members in the set. This yielded the per member giving amount in dollars. This per member giving amount was divided by per capita income. Disposable personal income was used since this after-tax figure eliminated the variation in taxes paid during any time period under consideration.

Data Appendix and Revisions. Appendix B includes the 1968 through 1994 data used in the analyses in this study. In general, the data for the denominations included in these analyses appears as it was reported in editions of the *YACC*. In some cases, data for one or more years for a specific denomination was obtained directly from the denominational office or another denominational source. Also, the denominational giving data set has been refined and revised as additional information has become available. Where relevant, this information is noted in the appendix.

1

Church Member Giving, 1968-1994 _____

There are perhaps few more objective measures of religious devotion than how much of one's income one invests in one's faith. Membership and attendance also provide indications. However, in this culture of accumulation that defines the United States at the end of the millennium, money can function as a thermometer of the heart's condition.

This idea is actually as old as the faith itself. In the Sermon on the Mount, Jesus Christ stated that "where your treasure is, there your heart will be also" (Matthew 6:21). One may therefore conclude that giving patterns provide an important measure of how much church members value their faith.

Twenty-nine Denominations. The present report is the seventh in a series that has tracked giving patterns in a set of Protestant communions in the U.S. that span the theological spectrum. The first study was published in 1988. It considered a set of 31 denominations for which church member giving data was published for 1968 and 1985 in the *Yearbook of American and Canadian Churches (YACC)*.[1] The data year 1968 was selected because, beginning that year, a consistent distinction was made between Full or Confirmed Membership and Inclusive Membership in the *YACC* series. These denominations included 29,442,390 Full or Confirmed Members in 1985, and comprised approximately 100,000 of the estimated 350,000 religious congregations in the U.S.

Following editions in the church member giving report series extended the analysis for the original set of denominations beyond 1985. The current report analyzes the data set, now comprising 29 denominations, through 1994, the most recent year for which data was available at the time the report was written.[2] Also, data for the intervening years of 1969

_____

[1] John Ronsvalle and Sylvia Ronsvalle, *A Comparison of the Growth in Church Contributions with United States Per Capita Income* (Champaign, IL: empty tomb, inc., 1988).
[2] Two of the original 31 denominations merged in 1987, bringing the total number of denominations in the original data set to 30. As of 1991, one denomination reported that it no longer had the staff to collect national data, resulting in a maximum of 29 denominations from the original set which could provide data for 1991 through 1994. Therefore, throughout this report, what was an original set of 31 denominations in 1985 will be referred to as a set of 29 denominations, reflecting the denominations' 1994 composition, although data for 31 denominations will be included for 1968 and 1985, as well as for intervening years, as available.

through 1984 was included in the composite data set, as available.[3]

The data yields the following observations for the denominations considered in this analysis.

Church Giving in Current Dollars. Church member giving can be considered from two perspectives. One might discuss the number of dollars a member gives to the church. The second approach would be to consider the portion, or percentage, of income that members donate to the church.

When considering the first option, the number of dollars donated, there are, in fact, two aspects to this category: current dollars (the value the dollars had in the year they were donated); and constant dollars (dollars that have been adjusted to factor out inflation, and thus can be compared across years).

Table 1 presents the data for the per member contribution in dollars for the composite group of denominations included in the data set. The data is considered in three categories. Total Contributions Per Member represents the average total contribution for each full or confirmed church member in the composite of 29 denominations. This Total Contributions figure is comprised of two subcategories: Congregational Finances (which includes the monies the congregation spent on internal operations); and Benevolences (which includes what might be termed the larger mission of the church, such as local, national and international missions, as well as denominational support and seminary funding, among other items).

During the period 1968 through 1994, the per member amount given to Total Contributions increased in current dollars each year. The part of Total Contributions Per Member which stayed in the congregation to fund Congregational Finances also went up each year. Per member contributions in current dollars directed to Benevolences also increased each year between 1968 and 1994, except from 1969 to 1970, when there was a decrease of $0.35.

The change in current dollar contributions displays a varied pattern from year to year. For example, the largest current dollar change in Total Contributions Per Member occurred from 1980 to 1981, when the amount increased $23.17. However, the largest increase to Congregational Finances in current dollars was from 1983 to 1984, when per member contributions to that category increased $19.86. Benevolences had the highest annual change in per member contributions between 1980 to 1981, the same year as Total Contributions. The year 1981 measured $4.80 more in per member contributions to Benevolences than in 1980.

As already noted, the only decline in per member giving in current dollars occurred

---

[3] For 1986 through 1994, annual denominational data has been obtained which represented for any given year at least 99.52% of the 1985 Full or Confirmed Membership of the denominations included in the 1968-1985 study, and the number of denominations for which data was available varied from a low of 25 in 1986 to a high of 29 in 1991 through 1994. The denominational giving data considered in this analysis was obtained either from the *Yearbook of American and Canadian Churches* series, or directly in correspondence with a denominational office. For a full listing of the data used in this analysis, including the sources, see Appendix A.

Table 1: **Per Member Giving to Total Contributions, Congregational Finances and Benevolences, Current and Constant 1987 Dollars, 1968-1994**

	Per Full or Confirmed Member Giving to Congregations, in Dollars								
	Current Dollars			Constant 1987 Dollars					
Year	Total	Cong. Finances	Benevol.	Total	↑↓	Cong. Finances	↑↓	Benevol.	↑↓
1968	*$96.58*	*$76.21*	*$20.37*	$308.57		$243.50		$65.07	
1969	*$100.63*	*$79.03*	*$21.60*	$305.86	↓	$240.21	↓	$65.64	↑
1970	*$103.82*	*$82.57*	*$21.25*	$299.20	↓	$237.97	↓	$61.23	↓
1971	*$109.43*	*$86.92*	*$22.51*	$299.00	↓	$237.49	↓	$61.51	↑
1972	*$116.91*	*$93.08*	*$23.83*	$304.46	↑	$242.40	↑	$62.06	↑
1973	*$127.23*	*$101.87*	*$25.36*	$311.08	↑	$249.07	↑	$62.01	↓
1974	*$138.74*	*$110.64*	*$28.10*	$313.17	↑	$249.74	↑	$63.43	↑
1975	*$149.93*	*$118.17*	*$31.76*	$308.50	↓	$243.15	↓	$65.36	↑
1976	*$162.63*	*$128.88*	*$33.75*	$314.57	↑	$249.28	↑	$65.29	↓
1977	*$175.40*	*$139.79*	*$35.61*	$316.61	↑	$252.32	↑	$64.29	↓
1978	*$192.57*	*$154.26*	*$38.31*	$321.49	↑	$257.54	↑	$63.96	↓
1979	*$211.15*	*$169.17*	*$41.98*	$323.84	↑	$259.46	↑	$64.39	↑
1980	*$231.90*	*$185.59*	*$46.32*	$326.63	↑	$261.39	↑	$65.24	↑
1981	*$255.08*	*$203.96*	*$51.12*	$329.13	↑	$263.18	↑	$65.96	↑
1982	*$275.73*	*$223.22*	*$52.51*	$334.62	↑	$270.90	↑	$63.72	↓
1983	*$292.62*	*$236.47*	*$56.15*	$339.47	↑	$274.33	↑	$65.13	↑
1984	*$315.34*	*$256.34*	*$59.01*	$349.22	↑	$283.87	↑	$65.34	↑
1985	*$335.63*	*$272.55*	*$63.08*	$357.81	↑	$290.56	↑	$67.25	↑
1986	*$352.84*	*$287.50*	*$65.33*	$365.26	↑	$297.62	↑	$67.63	↑
1987	*$367.23*	*$300.67*	*$66.57*	$367.23	↑	$300.67	↑	$66.57	↓
1988	*$381.92*	*$312.13*	*$69.79*	$367.23	↔	$300.13	↓	$67.11	↑
1989	*$403.02*	*$330.18*	*$72.84*	$370.77	↑	$303.75	↑	$67.01	↓
1990	*$419.52*	*$345.53*	*$73.99*	$369.62	↓	$304.43	↑	$65.19	↓
1991	*$433.69*	*$357.96*	*$75.73*	$368.79	↓	$304.39	↓	$64.40	↓
1992	*$445.16*	*$367.42*	*$77.74*	$366.39	↓	$302.40	↓	$63.99	↓
1993	*$457.72*	*$379.82*	*$77.91*	$367.35	↑	$304.83	↑	$62.53	↓
1994	*$477.21*	*$396.99*	*$80.22*	$375.46	↑	$312.34	↑	$63.11	↑

Details in the above table may not compute to the numbers shown due to rounding.

in Benevolences from 1969 to 1970, when per member giving decreased $0.35. The per member contribution in current dollars to Total Contributions posted an increase of $19.48 from 1993 to 1994, the sixth largest increase in the 1968-1994 period. Per member giving to Congregational Finances increased by $17.17, and to Benevolences by $2.31 from 1993 to 1994.

Church Giving in Constant Dollars. When the effects of inflation were factored out by applying a deflator, to convert the data to constant 1987 dollars, the analysis produced different results. During the 26-year interval from 1968 to 1994, Total Contributions Per

Member went up in 18 years, and held constant from 1987 to 1988. In the other seven years—1969, 1970, 1971, 1975, 1990, 1991 and 1992—Total Contributions in constant 1987 dollars declined per member from the previous year.

Congregational Finances increased from one year to the next except in seven years—in 1969, 1970, 1971, 1975, 1988, 1991 and 1992—when per member contributions in constant 1987 dollars decreased from the previous year.

Benevolences increased fourteen times and demonstrated a decline in per member contributions in constant 1987 dollars in twelve of the 26 two-year sets in the interval. There was a decline from the previous year in the per member amount of contributions for Benevolences in 1970, 1973, 1976, 1977 1978, 1982, 1987, 1989, 1990, 1991, 1992 and 1993.

As noted above, Table 1 presents per member figures for Total Contributions, Congregational Finances and Benevolences in current dollars and constant 1987 dollars. The arrows next to each constant dollar category indicate whether the dollar amount contributed to a given category increased or decreased from the previous year.

A study of the Table 1 constant dollar columns yields the following information. The most common pattern was for all three constant dollar categories to increase. In ten years—1972, 1974, 1979, 1980, 1981, 1983, 1984, 1985, 1986 and 1994—each of the three categories posted more constant dollars from the previous year.

The second most common pattern was for gifts to Total Contributions and Congregational Finances to increase while gifts to Benevolences decreased. This combination was found in eight years: 1973, 1976, 1977, 1978, 1982, 1987, 1989 and 1993.

In three years, Total Contributions and Congregational Finances decreased in constant dollars while Benevolences went up. These years were 1969, 1971 and 1975.

In three years, constant dollar contributions to all three categories decreased. This overall decrease occurred in 1970, 1991 and 1992.

In 1988, Total Contributions did not change, while the per member contribution to Congregational Finances went down and Benevolences went up.

In 1990, Total Contributions and Benevolences decreased in constant dollars while Congregational Finances increased.

Twice, a decrease in per member constant 1987 dollar contributions to Total Contributions occurred three years in a row during this 27-year period. This decrease happened in 1969, 1970 and 1971, and more recently in 1990, 1991 and 1992.

The increase of $2.31 to Benevolences between 1993 and 1994 was the first time per member gifts in constant dollars had increased to that category since 1988. The decline from 1989 through 1993 was the longest uninterrupted decrease in per member gifts to Benevolences in the 1968 to 1994 period.

It may also be noted that only in 1991 and 1992 did the constant 1987 dollar per member contributions decline to all three categories two years in a row. The year 1970 is the only other single year to post a constant 1987 dollar per member decrease to all three categories.

Figure 1: **Patterns in Per Member Giving—Changes in Per Member Giving in Constant 1987 Dollars among Total Contributions, Congregational Finances and Benevolences, 1968-1994**

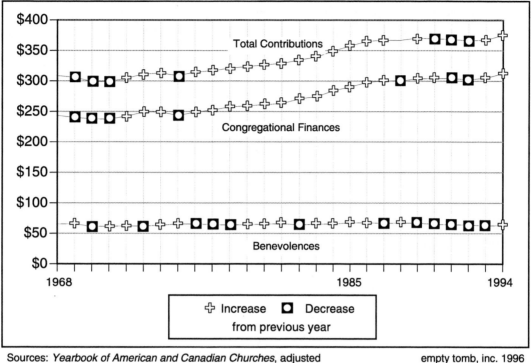

Sources: *Yearbook of American and Canadian Churches*, adjusted series; U.S. Bureau of Economic Analysis

empty tomb, inc. 1996

Figure 1 presents the changes in constant dollar contributions to these three categories in chart form.

Per member constant 1987 dollar contributions to Total Contributions increased $66.89 between 1968 and 1994. This $66.89 increase represented a 22% increase from the 1968 base, from $308.57 in 1968 to $375.46 in 1994.

This 22% increase in per member Total Contributions can be compared to the 54% increase in U.S. per capita disposable (after-tax) personal income during the same period, which increased from $9,831 in 1968 to $15,148 in 1994 in constant 1987 dollars.

Congregational Finances increased $68.85 per member between 1968 and 1994, or $1.95 (rounded) more than per member Total Contributions increased. Congregational Finances increased 28% from the 1968 base in constant 1987 dollar per member contributions compared to the 22% increase in Total Contributions noted above.

Benevolences therefore subsidized the increase in Congregational Finances. In 1968, per member contributions to Benevolences in constant 1987 dollars were $65.07. In 1994, this per member contribution had declined to $63.11, an amount of $1.95, representing a 3% decrease from the 1968 base.

The largest constant dollar increase in Total Contributions Per Member occurred between 1983 and 1984, when that amount went up $9.75. The largest decrease occurred between 1969 and 1970, when per member contributions to Total Contributions decreased

$6.66. The increase between 1993 and 1994 is the third largest increase in the 1968-1994 period.

The largest increase in per member contributions in constant dollars to Congregational Finances also occurred between 1983 and 1984, when contributions went up $9.54. The largest decrease occurred between 1974 and 1975, when per member contributions decreased $6.60. The increase of $7.52 between 1993 and 1994 is the third largest increase in the 1968-1994 period.

The largest increase in per member contributions in constant dollars to Benevolences occurred from 1974 to 1975, when per member contributions to Benevolences increased $1.93. The largest single decrease to Benevolences in constant dollars was from 1969 to 1970, when per member contributions decreased $4.41. Per member contributions to Benevolences decreased five years in a row, from 1989 through 1993. The cumulative decrease of these five years was $4.58, $0.17 more than the single-year decrease from 1969 to 1970 of $4.41. For the first time in six years, per member giving to Benevolences increased from 1993 to 1994, in the amount of $0.59. Gifts to Benevolences increased in 14 years, and decreased in 12 during the 1968 to 1994 period.

Figure 2 provides a comparison of per member giving to the categories of Congregational Finances and Benevolences with changes in U.S. per capita disposable personal income in constant 1987 dollars.

Figure 2:   Per Member Giving to Congregational Finances and Benevolences, and U.S. Per Capita Personal Income, 1968-1994, Constant 1987 Dollars

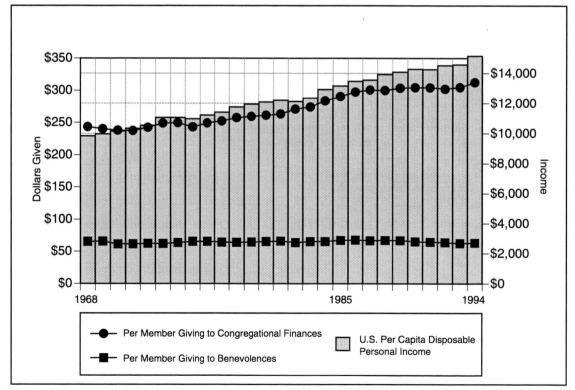

Sources: *Yearbook of American and Canadian Churches*, adjusted series; U.S. Bureau of Economic Analysis

empty tomb, inc. 1996

Giving as a Percent of Income. The second approach to considering per member giving to churches is the portion of income donated to the church. Individuals choose to spend their incomes to support their lifestyles in a variety of ways; and those incomes have changed over the years, apart from how inflation has affected the dollar. The real growth in the economy is reflected in the fact that U.S. per capita income increased by 54% between 1968 and 1994, after taxes and inflation have been factored out.

U.S. per capita income, an average income figure for the U.S., serves as an average income figure for the broad spectrum of church members included in the composite of 29 denominations. The percentage of U.S. per capita income which church members donated to their congregations provides a measure of what portion of their available resources church members directed to religion, as represented by these church structures, from 1968 to 1994. Thus, giving as a percentage of income is one indicator of how religion in America fares in comparison to other lifestyle choices being made by church members.

In Table 2, giving as a percentage of income is presented for per member Total Contributions, and the related subcategories of Congregational Finances and Benevolences. As in Table 1 the arrows by each category indicate whether the percentage of income in that category increased or decreased from the previous year. Inasmuch as the percent figures are rounded to the second decimal place, the arrows indicate the direction of a slight increase or decrease also for those situations in which the percentage provided is the same numerical figure as the previous year.

While Table 1 presents data in both current and constant dollars, Table 2 lists a single set of data for giving as a percentage of income. There is no distinction between current or constant dollars when one is considering giving as a percentage of income. The same procedures are applied to both the giving and income dollar amounts when converting current dollars into constant dollars. As long as one compares current dollar giving to current dollar per capita income when calculating the percentage of income, and constant dollar giving to constant dollar per capita income while using the same deflator, the percentages of income will be the same.

A review of Table 2 yields the following information. The most common pattern, occurring in twelve of the 26 two-year combinations from 1968 to 1994, was for the percentage of income going to each of the three categories to decrease. This happened in 1969, 1970, 1971, 1973, 1977, 1978, 1979, 1984, 1988, 1990, 1992 and 1994.

The next most frequent pattern occurred in seven years—1972, 1976, 1986, 1987, 1989, 1991 and 1993—when both Total Contributions Per Member and Benevolences decreased, and Congregational Finances increased.

In four years—1975, 1980, 1981 and 1983— Benevolences increased while both Total Contributions and Congregational Finances decreased.

In two other years—1974 and 1985—Total Contributions Per Member, Congregational Finances and Benevolences all experienced an increase.

Finally, in 1982, both Total Contributions and Congregational Finances increased, while Benevolences decreased.

Table 2:   Per Member Giving as a Percentage of Income, 1968-1994

Per Full or Confirmed Member Giving to Congregations as a Percentage of Income						
Year	Total Contributions Per Member	↑↓	Congregational Finances	↑↓	Benevolences	↑↓
1968	3.14%		2.48%		0.66%	
1969	3.07%	↓	2.41%	↓	0.66%	↓
1970	2.95%	↓	2.35%	↓	0.60%	↓
1971	2.90%	↓	2.30%	↓	0.60%	↓
1972	2.89%	↓	2.30%	↑	0.59%	↓
1973	2.81%	↓	2.25%	↓	0.56%	↓
1974	2.84%	↑	2.26%	↑	0.57%	↑
1975	2.81%	↓	2.22%	↓	0.60%	↑
1976	2.81%	↓	2.22%	↑	0.58%	↓
1977	2.78%	↓	2.21%	↓	0.56%	↓
1978	2.73%	↓	2.19%	↓	0.54%	↓
1979	2.71%	↓	2.17%	↓	0.54%	↓
1980	2.70%	↓	2.16%	↓	0.54%	↑
1981	2.70%	↓	2.16%	↓	0.54%	↑
1982	2.76%	↑	2.23%	↑	0.53%	↓
1983	2.75%	↓	2.22%	↓	0.53%	↑
1984	2.70%	↓	2.20%	↓	0.51%	↓
1985	2.72%	↑	2.21%	↑	0.51%	↑
1986	2.71%	↓	2.21%	↑	0.50%	↓
1987	2.71%	↓	2.22%	↑	0.49%	↓
1988	2.64%	↓	2.16%	↓	0.48%	↓
1989	2.63%	↓	2.16%	↑	0.48%	↓
1990	2.59%	↓	2.13%	↓	0.46%	↓
1991	2.59%	↓	2.14%	↑	0.45%	↓
1992	2.52%	↓	2.08%	↓	0.44%	↓
1993	2.52%	↓	2.09%	↑	0.43%	↓
1994	2.48%	↓	2.06%	↓	0.42%	↓

Details in the above table may not compute to the numbers shown due to rounding.

Figure 3 presents changes in giving as a percentage of income for the categories of Congregational Finances and Benevolences and U.S. per capita disposable personal income.

In summary, out of the 26 two-year periods, giving as a percentage of income for Total Contributions Per Member decreased 23 times from the previous year between 1968 and 1994. The period 1986 through 1994 produced the longest decline in the portion of per capita income to Total Contributions in this 27-year period, posting declines nine years in a row.

Congregational Finances decreased 16 times and Benevolences decreased 20 times from the previous year during the same 26 two-year sets in the 1968-1994 period. The portion of income directed to Congregational Finances has alternately increased and decreased since

Figure 3: **Per Member Giving as a Percentage of Income to Congregational Finances and Benevolences, and U.S. Per Capita Disposable Personal Income, 1968-1994**

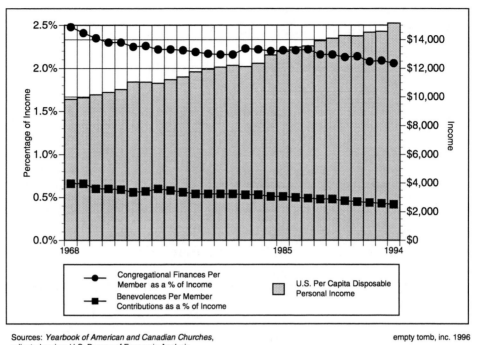

Sources: *Yearbook of American and Canadian Churches*, adjusted series; U.S. Bureau of Economic Analysis

empty tomb, inc. 1996

1987. As in Total Contributions, the portion of income to Benevolences declined nine years in a row from 1986 through 1994, the longest uninterrupted decline during this period.

During the 1968-1994 time frame, the percent change in giving as a percentage of income to Total Contributions declined by 21% from the 1968 base. During the same 26-year interval, U.S. per capita disposable personal income increased 54%.

Congregational Finances declined from 2.48% in 1968 to 2.06% in 1994, a percent decline of 17% from the 1968 base. Benevolences experienced the largest proportional decrease of the three categories. Per member contributions to Benevolences as a percentage of income declined from 0.66% in 1968 to 0.42% in 1994, a percent decline of 37% in the portion of income from the 1968 base.

Giving in Constant Dollars, 1968, 1985 and 1994. The initial report in this series on church member giving considered data for the denominations in the composite for the years 1968 and 1985. With the data now available through 1994, a broader trend can be reviewed for the period under discussion, the 27-year range from 1968 to 1994.

The amount donated to Total Contributions Per Member in constant 1987 dollars was $49.25 greater in 1985 than it was in 1968 for the denominations included in the first analysis, an average increase of $2.90 a year in per member contributions. There was an overall increase during the 1985-1994 eight-year interval, as well. In 1994, the per member contribution to the 29 denominations, which represented 99.84% of the total 1985 membership of the denominations originally studied, was $17.65 more per member in constant 1987 dollars than in 1985. The average annual increase was $1.96 between 1985 and 1994, compared to an average annual increase between 1968 and 1985 of $2.90.

15

Gifts to Congregational Finances also increased between 1968 and 1985, as well as from 1985 to 1994. However, as in the case of Total Contributions, the annual rate of increase declined. Per member contributions to Congregational Finances were $243.50 in 1968, in constant 1987 dollars, and had increased to $290.56 in 1985, a total increase of $47.07, with an average rate of change of $2.77. From 1985 to 1994, the average annual rate of change declined to $2.42, with per member gifts growing from $290.56 in 1985 to $312.34 in 1994, an increase of $21.78.

Benevolences experienced a reversal in the rate of change during the 1985 to 1994 period. In constant 1987 dollars, gifts to Benevolences were $65.07 in 1968 and grew to $67.25 in 1985, an increase of $2.18, with an annual average rate of change of $0.13. Between 1985 and 1994, per member gifts to Benevolences declined to $63.11 in 1994 from the 1985 level of $67.25, a decrease of $4.13, with an annual average rate of change of -$0.46 for the 1985-1994 period.

Table 3 presents per member gifts to Total Contributions, Congregational Finances and Benevolences in constant 1987 dollars for the years 1968, 1985 and 1994.

Table 3:   Total Contributions, Congregational Finances and Benevolences, Per Member Giving in Constant 1987 Dollars, 1968, 1985 and 1994

| | Per Member Giving in Constant 1987 Dollars | | | | | | | | |
| | Total Contributions | | | Congregational Finances | | | Benevolences | | |
Year	Per Member Giving in Constant '87 Dollars	Diff. from Previous Constant $ Base	Average Annual Diff. in $s Given	Per Member Giving in Constant '87 Dollars	Diff. from Previous Constant $ Base	Average Annual Diff. in $s Given	Per Member Giving in Constant '87 Dollars	Diff. from Previous Constant $ Base	Average Annual Diff. in $s Given
1968	$308.57			$243.50			$65.07		
1985	$357.81	$49.25	$2.90	$290.56	$47.07	$2.77	$67.25	$2.18	$0.13
1994	$375.46	$17.65	$1.96	$312.34	$21.78	$2.42	$63.11	-$4.13	-$0.46

Details in the above table may not compute to the numbers shown due to rounding.

Giving as a Percentage of Income, 1968, 1985 and 1994. As noted earlier, per member giving increased $66.89 between 1968 and 1994, an increase of 22% from the 1968 base in constant 1987 dollars. Also noted earlier, during the same 27-year period, U.S. per capita disposable personal income increased 54% in constant 1987 dollars, from $9,831 in 1968 to $15,148 in 1994.

The difference in the rate of increase between dollars contributed and per capita income explains how church member contributions could be increasing in constant dollars in more than half the years from 1968 to 1994, and yet decreasing as a percentage of income in more than half the years from 1968 to 1994.

Between 1968 and 1985, Total Contributions declined from 3.14% to 2.72% as a portion of income. The percentage change in giving as a percentage of income from the 1968 base was -13.34% in the 17 years from 1968 to 1985.

From 1985 to 1994, giving as a percentage of income to Total Contributions changed from 2.72% in 1985 to 2.48% in 1994, a difference of -0.24%. The percentage change in giving as a percentage of income from the 1985 base was -8.88% in this nine-year interval. Therefore, the annual percent change in the portion of per capita income donated to Total Contributions was -0.99% in the 1985-1994 period, compared to the rate of -0.78% in the 1968-1985 period.

Table 4 presents data for Total Contributions Per member as a percentage of income in summary fashion for the years 1968, 1985 and 1994.

Table 4: **Per Member Giving as a Percentage of Income to Total Contributions, 1968, 1985 and 1994**

	Total Contributions Per Member as a Percentage of Income			
Year	Total Contributions Per Member as a Percentage of Income	Difference in Total Contributions Per Member as a Percentage of Income from Previous Base	Percent Change in Total Contributions Per Member as a Percentage of Income from Previous Base	Annual Average Percent Change in Total Contributions Per Member as a Percentage of Income
1968	3.14%			
1985	2.72%	-0.42%	-13.34% from 1968 base	-0.78%
1994	2.48%	-0.24%	-8.88% from 1985 base	-0.99%

Details in the above table may not compute to the numbers shown due to rounding.

Per member gifts to Congregational Finances measured 2.48% of income in 1968, 2.21% in 1985 and 2.06% in 1994. The annual average percent change in giving as a percentage of income changed from -0.64% a year between 1968 and 1985 from the 1968 base to -0.74% a year between 1985 and 1994 from the 1985 base. Table 5 presents this data.

Table 5: **Per Member Giving as a Percentage of Income to Congregational Finances, 1968, 1985 and 1994**

	Congregational Finances Per Member as a Percentage of Income			
Year	Cong. Finances Per Member as a Percentage of Income	Difference in Cong. Finances Per Member as a Percentage of Income from Previous Base	Percent Change in Cong. Finances Per Member as a Percentage of Income from Previous Base	Annual Average Percent Change in Cong. Finances Per Member as a Percentage of Income
1968	2.48%			
1985	2.21%	-0.27%	-10.82% from 1968 base	-0.64%
1994	2.06%	-0.15%	-6.65% from 1985 base	-0.74%

Details in the above table may not compute to the numbers shown due to rounding

The annual average percent change in giving as a percentage of income to Benevolences accelerated between 1985 and 1994, compared to the 1968-1985 period. From 1968 to 1985, the portion of member income directed to Benevolences decreased from 0.66% to

0.51%, a decline of 0.15%. This translated to a percent change in giving as a percentage of income of -22.77% from the 1968 base, with an annual average percent change of -1.34%. In the nine-year interval from 1985 to 1994, the percent change in giving as a percentage of income was more than half of the 17-year interval percent change from 1968-1985. Giving as a percentage of income directed to Benevolences declined from 0.51% to 0.42%, a percent change in giving as a percentage of income of -18.50% from the 1985 base, with an annual average percent change of -2.06%. Table 6 presents the data for Benevolences as a percentage of income in 1968, 1985 and 1994.

Table 6:   Per Member Giving as a Percentage of Income to Benevolences, 1968, 1985 and 1994

Benevolences Per Member as a Percentage of Income				
Year	Benevolences Per Member as a Percentage of Income	Difference in Benevolences Per Member as a Percentage of Income from Previous Base	Percent Change in Benevolences Per Member as a Percentage of Income from Previous Base	Annual Average Percent Change in Benevolences Per Member as a Percentage of Income
1968	0.66%			
1985	0.51%	-0.15%	-22.77% from 1968 base	-1.34%
1994	0.42%	-0.09%	-18.50% from 1985 base	-2.06%

Details in the above table may not compute to the numbers shown due to rounding.

Giving in 1993 Compared to 1994. Per member giving as a percentage of income to Total Contributions in 1993 measured 2.52%. In 1994, the figure was 2.48%.

Congregational Finances continued a pattern of alternately decreasing and increasing from year to year. From 1993 to 1994, Congregational Finances decreased from 2.09% to 2.06%, a decrease of 1.45% from the 1993 base. This decrease followed an increase from 1992 to 1993 from 2.08% to 2.09%.

From 1993 to 1994, Benevolences extended a multiyear pattern of decline, changing from 0.43% in 1993 to 0.42% in 1994, a decline of 2.92% from the 1993 base.

Potential Giving. Apart from the question of whether church members could have been giving a higher percentage of their incomes in 1994 than in 1968, what would have been the situation in 1994 if giving had at least maintained the 1968 percentages of income donated? Rather than the actual 1994 levels of giving, what if giving as a percentage of income in 1994 measured 3.14% for Total Contributions, 2.48% for Congregational Finances, and 0.66% for Benevolences, which were the levels of giving for these three categories in 1968?

Had that been true, per member giving to Total Contributions in current 1994 dollars would have been $604.44 instead of $477.21; Congregational Finances would have been $477.03 instead of $396.99; and Benevolences would have been $127.41 instead of $80.22.

The implications of these differences becomes clearer when the aggregate totals are calculated by multiplying the theoretical per member giving levels by the number of members reported by these denominations in 1994. Aggregate Total Contributions would then have been $18.0 billion rather than $14.2 billion, a difference of $3.8 billion, or an increase of 27%.

Aggregate Congregational Finances would have been $14.2 billion rather than $11.8 billion, a difference of $2.4 billion, or an increase of 20%.

There would have been a 59% increase in the total amount received for Benevolences. Instead of receiving $2.4 billion in 1994, as these denominations did, they would have received $3.8 billion, a difference of $1.4 billion.

Summary. Church member giving, considered in current dollars, generally increased between 1968 and 1994. This was true for Total Contributions as well as Congregational Finances. The only exception in Benevolences was the decrease in current dollar giving between 1969 and 1970.

When inflation was factored out, Total Contributions posted an overall increase in the amount of constant 1987 dollars donated per member from 1968 to 1994. The per member contribution to Congregational Finances increased more than the additional Total Contributions received between 1968 and 1994. Benevolences experienced a decrease in the per member contribution received, amounting to $1.95 less in 1994 than in 1968 in constant 1987 dollars.

When giving as a percentage of income was considered, an overall decline in each of the three categories of Total Contributions, Congregational Finances and Benevolences from 1968 to 1994 was observed. Of the three categories, Benevolences experienced the largest proportional decrease.

2

Church Member Giving for
47 Denominations, 1993 to 1994

The composite group of denominations studied in this church member giving series was limited to 29 communions because other historically Christian denominations in the U.S. had not published data for 1968 and 1985, the years of the first study in the series. However, eighteen other denominations did publish data for both 1993 and 1994. By adding the data for these 18 denominations to that of the composite group for these two years, giving patterns in a broader spectrum of the church can be considered.

In this enlarged comparison, the member sample increased from approximately 30 million to 41 million Full or Confirmed Members, and the number of denominations increased from 29 to 47. The larger group of denominations included both The United Methodist Church and The Episcopal Church, which were not included in the original 1968-1985 analysis because of the unavailability of confirmed 1968 data.[4] A list of the denominations included in the analysis is contained in Appendix A.

Per Member Giving in Constant Dollars. As noted in the first chapter of this report, per member giving to Total Contributions posted an increase from 1993 to 1994 for the composite group of 29 denominations in constant 1987 dollars. Specifically, Total Contributions Per Member increased by $8.10 in constant 1987 dollars from 1993 to 1994, from $367.35 in 1993 to $375.46 in 1994. When the group was expanded to 47 denominations, Total Per Member giving increased by $8.83 from 1993 to 1994, from $378.49 in 1993 to $387.32 in 1994.

The composite group of 29 denominations increased per member giving in constant dollars to Congregational Finances by $7.52, from $304.83 in 1993 to $312.34 in 1994. The expanded group increased by $8.29, from $311.39 in 1993 to $319.68 in 1994. In both the sets of 29 denominations and 47 denominations, the per member increase to Total Contributions was larger than the increase to Congregational Finances. Thus, for both groups, Benevolences posted an increase: in the composite of 29 communions from $62.53 to $63.11, an increase of $0.59; and in the expanded group of 47 denominations, from $67.10 to $67.64, an increase of $0.54.

---

[4] The denominational giving data considered in this analysis was obtained from the *Yearbook of American and Canadian Churches*, except as noted in the appendices.

It may be noted that although the per member giving increase to Total Contributions in constant 1987 dollars was larger in the expanded group of 47 denominations than it was in the composite of 29 denominations, the increase to Benevolences was smaller in the expanded group of 47 than in the composite of 29.

Per Member Giving as a Percentage of Income. In the 1968-1994 composite of 29 denominations, giving as a percentage of income declined to Total Contributions, Congregational Finances and Benevolences from 1993 to 1994. That is, in the composite group of 29 denominations, the percent given to Total Contributions measured a decline from 2.52% in 1993 to 2.48% in 1994; Congregational Finances decreased from 2.09% to 2.06%; and Benevolences changed from 0.43% to 0.42%.

In the expanded group of 47 denominations, giving as a percentage of income also decreased to Total Contributions and the two subcategories of Congregational Finances and Benevolences. In this expanded set, the percent of per capita income given on a per member basis to Total Contributions measured 2.67% in 1993 and 2.56% in 1994; Congregational Finances decreased from 2.20% to 2.11%; and Benevolences declined from 0.47% to 0.45%.

The rate of percent change in giving as a percentage of income for the composite group of 29 denominations was -1.70% from the 1993 base for Total Contributions, compared to -4.38% for the expanded group of 47 denominations. For Congregational Contributions, the composite group of 29 denominations posted a rate of -1.45% percent change in giving as a percentage of income from the 1993 base, compared to -4.07% for the expanded group of 47 denominations. Benevolences for the composite group of 29 denominations posted a -2.92% percent change in giving as a percentage of income from the 1993 base, compared to a rate of -5.81% for the expanded group of 47 denominations.

Membership, 1993-1994. The Full or Confirmed Membership in the expanded group of 47 denominations increased from 1993 to 1994. In 1993, these 47 communions reported 40,777,796 members. In 1994, these same denominations reported 40,782,292 members, an increase of 4,496. This compares with a membership change in the 29 composite denominations from 29,705,072 in 1993 to 29,765,898, an increase of 60,826.

Table 7 presents membership, as well as per member giving data for 1993 and 1994 for the expanded group of 47 denominations in constant 1987 dollars, and as a percentage of income. In addition, the change from 1993 to 1994 in membership, in per member contributions in constant 1987 dollars, in giving as a percentage of income, and in the percent change in giving as a percentage of income from the 1993 base are also presented in the table.

Summary. When the data set of 29 denominations was expanded to include an additional 18 denominations, bringing the total to 47, approximately eleven million additional members were added to the data set. In both the composite of 29 denominations and the expanded group of 47 denominations, per member giving in constant 1987 dollars increased to Total Contributions, Congregational Finances and Benevolences from 1993-1994.

Giving as a percentage of income decreased to Total Contributions, Congregational Finances, and Benevolences for the expanded group of 47 denominations. This same pattern was evident in the composite of 29 denominations.

Table 7: **Per Member Giving in 47 Denominations, 1993 and 1994, in Constant 1987 Dollars and as a Percentage of Income**

Year	Full or Confirmed Membership	Total Contributions Per Member		Congregational Finances		Benevolences	
		$s Given in Constant '87 Dollars	Giving as % of Income	$s Given in Constant '87 Dollars	Giving as % of Income	$s Given in Constant '87 Dollars	Giving as % of Income
1993	40,777,796	$378.49	2.67%	$311.39	2.20%	$67.10	0.47%
1994	40,782,292	$387.32	2.56%	$319.68	2.11%	$67.64	0.45%
Difference from the 1993 Base	4,496	$8.83	-0.11%	$8.29	-0.09%	$0.54	-0.02%
% Change in Giving as % of Income from the 1993 Base			-4.38%		-4.07%		-5.81%

Details in the above table may not compute to the numbers shown due to rounding

3

Church Member Giving in Denominations Defined by Organizational Affiliation———————

The 1968-1994 data analysis for the composite of 29 denominations shows that church giving as a percentage of income declined between the years 1968 and 1994. The area of Benevolences showed the largest proportional decrease.

In order to observe whether this trend is common across the theological spectrum, or limited to only certain traditions, two subsets of denominations in the composite group of 29 communions can be identified. These groupings may provide insight into a long-standing assumption, that church members who might be termed "evangelical" give more money to their churches than do church members who belong to what are often termed mainline Protestant denominations.

In the composite group of 29 denominations, eight communions for which financial data is available for 1968, 1985 and 1994 were affiliated with the National Association of Evangelicals (NAE). Eight denominations affiliated with the National Council of the Churches of Christ in the U.S.A. (NCC) also had financial data available for 1968, 1985 and 1994.

Of course, there is diversity of opinion within any denomination, as well as in multi-communion groupings such as the NAE or the NCC. For purposes of the present analysis, however, these two groups may serve as general categories, since they have been characterized as representing certain types of denominations. For example, the National Association of Evangelicals has, by choice of its title, defined its denominational constituency. And traditionally, the National Council of the Churches of Christ in the U.S.A. has counted among its members many of the mainline denominations.

Recognizing that there are limitations in defining a denomination's theological perspectives merely by membership in one of these two organizations, a review of giving patterns of the two subsets of denominations, totaling 16 communions within the larger composite of 29 denominations, may nevertheless provide some insight into how widely spread declining giving patterns may be. Therefore, an analysis of 1968-1994 giving patterns was completed for the two subsets of those denominations which were affiliated with one of these two interdenominational organizations.

Using 1985 data, the eight denominations affiliated with the NAE as of 1994 represented 18% of the total number of NAE-member denominations as listed in the *Yearbook of American and Canadian Churches (YACC)* series; 21% of the total number of NAE-member denominations with membership data listed in the *YACC*; and approximately 21% of the total membership of the NAE-member denominations with membership data listed in the *YACC*.[5] As noted in Table 8, per member giving as a percentage of income to Total Contributions for a composite of those eight NAE-member denominations was 6.19% in 1968.

Data was also available for eight NCC-member denominations in the larger composite group of 29 denominations. Originally, ten of the denominations studied for 1968-1985 were members of the NCC. Two of these denominations merged in 1987, bringing the number of NCC-affiliated denominations in the larger composite to nine communions. Tellingly, another denomination in this original grouping no longer has the staff to compile national data, and therefore is not included in the analysis through 1994, bringing to eight the number of NCC-member denominations in the composite of 29 which had available data for 1968-1994. In 1985, these eight denominations represented 27% of the total number of NCC constituent bodies as listed in the *YACC*; 30% of the NCC constituent bodies with membership data listed in the *YACC*; and approximately 29% of the total membership of the NCC constituent bodies with membership data listed in the *YACC*.[6] As noted in Table 8, in

Table 8: **Per Member Giving as a Percentage of Income to Total Contributions in Eight NAE and Eight NCC Denominations, 1968, 1985 and 1994**

	Total Contributions										
	NAE Denominations					NCC Denominations					
Year	Number of Denom. Analyzed	Total Contrib. Per Member as % of Income	Diff. in Total Contrib. Per Member as % of Income from Previous Base	Percent Change in Total Contrib. as % of Income from Previous Base	Avg. Annual % Change in Total Contrib. as % of Income from Previous Base	Number of Denom. Analyzed	Total Contrib. Per Member as % of Income	Diff. in Total Contrib. Per Member as % of Income from Previous Base	Percent Change in Total Contrib. as % of Income from Previous Base	Avg. Annual % Change in Total Contrib. as % of Income from Previous Base
1968	8	6.19%				8	3.35%			
1985	8	4.95%	-1.24%	-19.95% from '68 base	-1.17%	8	2.99%	-0.36%	-10.74% from '68 base	-0.63%
1994	8	4.16%	-0.79%	-16.03% from '85 base	-1.78%	8	2.93%	-0.06%	-2.01% from '85 base	-0.22%

Details in the above table may not compute to the numbers shown due to rounding.

---

[5] The 1985 total church membership estimate of 3,388,414 represented by NAE denominations includes *YACC* 1985 membership data for each denomination where available or, if 1985 membership data was not available, membership data for the most recent year prior to 1985. Full or Confirmed membership data was used or, in those instances where this figure was not available, Inclusive Membership was used.
[6] The 1985 total church membership estimate of 39,621,950 represented by NCC denominations includes *YACC* 1985 membership data for each denomination where available or, if 1985 membership data was not available, membership data for the most recent year prior to 1985. Full or Confirmed membership data was used or, in those instances where this figure was not available, Inclusive Membership was used.

1968, per member giving as a percentage of income to Total Contributions was 3.35% for a composite of these eight NCC denominations.

In 1985, the NAE denominations' per member giving as a percentage of income level was 4.95%, while the NCC level was 2.99%.

The data shows the NAE-member denominations received a larger portion of their members' incomes than did NCC-affiliated denominations in both 1968 and 1985. This information supports the assumption that denominations identifying with an evangelical perspective received a higher level of support than denominations that may be termed mainline.

The analysis also presents another finding. The decline in levels of giving observed in the larger composite of 29 denominations was also evident among both the NAE-member denominations and the NCC-member denominations. While giving levels decreased for both sets of denominations between 1968 and 1985, the decrease was more pronounced in the NAE-affiliated communions in Total Contributions. The percent change in percentage of income donated in the NAE-member denominations, in comparison to the 1968 base, declined 20% between 1968 and 1985, while the percent change in percentage of income given to the NCC-member denominations declined 11%.

Thus, although the evangelical church members continued to give more than mainline church members, the difference in giving levels was smaller in 1985 than in 1968.

Changes in Giving, 1985-1994. A decline in giving as a percentage of income continued among the eight NAE-member denominations during the 1985-1994 period. By 1994, per member giving as a percentage of income to Total Contributions had declined from the 1985 level of 4.95% to 4.16%, a percentage drop of 16% from the 1985 base in the portion of members' incomes donated over that nine-year interval.

Meanwhile, the eight NCC-affiliated denominations also declined in giving as a percentage of income to Total Contributions during 1985-1994, from the 1985 level of 2.99% to 2.93% in 1994, a percentage decline of 2% from the 1985 base in the portion of income given to these churches.

Because of the decline in the portion of income given in the NAE-affiliated denominations, in 1994 the difference in per member giving as a percentage of income between the NAE-affiliated denominations and the NCC-affiliated denominations was not as large as it had been in 1968. Comparing the two rates in giving as a percentage of income to Total Contributions between the NAE-member denominations and the NCC-member denominations in this analysis, the NCC-affiliated denominations received 54% as much of per member income as the NAE-member denominations did in 1968, 60% as much in 1985, and 70% in 1994.

For the NAE-affiliated denominations, during the 1985 to 1994 period, the rate of decrease in the average annual percent change in per member giving as a percentage of income to Total Contributions, from the 1985 base, accelerated in comparison to the 1968-1985 annual percent change from the 1968 base. The 1968-1985 average annual percent change was -1.17%. The figure for 1985-1994 was -1.78%.

In the NCC-member denominations, the trend slowed. While the average annual percent change from the 1968 base in giving as a percentage of income was -0.63% between 1968 and 1985, the average annual change from the 1985 base was -0.22% between 1985 and 1994.

Congregational Finances and Benevolences Giving. Were there any markedly different patterns between the two subsets of denominations defined by affiliation with the NAE and the NCC in regards to the distribution of Total Contributions between the subcategories of Congregational Finances and Benevolences?

In fact, both subsets of communions displayed the same trend noted in the composite group of 29 denominations. Between 1968 and 1994, both categories of Congregational Finances and Benevolences declined as a percentage of income in the NCC-affiliated denominations as well as in the NAE-affiliated group. It may be noted, however, that the NCC-related denominations showed an increase in the percentage of income donated to Congregational Finances in the 1985 to 1994 period.

Table 9 presents the Congregational Finances giving data for the NAE and NCC denominations in 1968, 1985 and 1994.

Table 9: **Per Member Giving as a Percentage of Income to Congregational Finances in Eight NAE and Eight NCC Denominations, 1968, 1985 and 1994**

	Congregational Finances									
	NAE Denominations					NCC Denominations				
Year	Number of Denom. Analyzed	Cong. Finances Per Member as % of Income	Diff. in Cong. Finances Per Member as % of Income from Previous Base	Percent Change in Cong. Finances as % of Income from Previous Base	Avg. Annual % Change in Cong. Finances as % of Income from Previous Base	Number of Denom. Analyzed	Cong. Finances Per Member as % of Income	Diff. in Cong. Finances Per Member as % of Income from Previous Base	Percent Change in Cong. Finances as % of Income from Previous Base	Avg. Annual % Change in Cong. Finances as % of Income from Previous Base
1968	8	5.03%				8	2.71%			
1985	8	3.99%	-1.04%	-20.70% from '68 base	-1.22%	8	2.52%	-0.19%	-6.94% from '68 base	-0.41%
1994	8	3.40%	-0.59%	-14.77% from '85 base	-1.64%	8	2.55%	0.03%	1.00% from '85 base	0.11%

Details in the above table may not compute to the numbers shown due to rounding.

Table 10 presents the Benevolences giving data for the NAE and NCC denominations in 1968, 1985 and 1994.

The previous edition in *The State of Church Giving* series indicated the NAE-affiliated denominations had declined 18.42% between 1985 and 1993 in giving as a percentage of income to Benevolences, compared to -16.70% between 1968 and 1985. Thus, the rate of giving had declined more in the eight-year period from 1985-1993 than in the earlier 17-year period from 1968-1985.

Table 10 indicates the trend continued in 1994, with a 21.27% decline in the nine years between 1985 and 1994.

Table 10: **Per Member Giving as a Percentage of Income to Benevolences in Eight NAE and Eight NCC Denominations, 1968, 1985 and 1994**

| | Benevolences | | | | | | | | | | |
| | NAE Denominations | | | | | NCC Denominations | | | | | |
Year	Number of Denom. Analyzed	Benevol. Per Member as % of Income	Diff. in Benevol. Per Member as % of Income from Previous Base	Percent Change in Benevol. as % of Income from Previous Base	Avg. Annual % Chng. in Benevol. as % of Income from Previous Base	Number of Denom. Analyzed	Benevol. Per Member as % of Income	Diff. in Benevol. Per Member as % of Income from Previous Base	Percent Change in Benevol. as % of Income from Previous Base	Avg. Annual % Chng. in Benevol. as % of Income from Previous Base
1968	8	1.16%				8	0.64%			
1985	8	0.96%	-0.20%	-16.70% from '68 base	-0.98%	8	0.47%	-0.17%	-26.91% from '68 base	-1.58%
1994	8	0.76%	-0.20%	-21.27% from '85 base	-2.36%	8	0.38%	-0.09%	-18.38% from '85 base	-2.04%

Details in the above table may not compute to the numbers shown due to rounding.

For the NCC-affiliated denominations, between 1968 and 1994, per member giving as a percentage of income declined 6% decline from the 1968 base in the subcategory of Congregational Finances, compared to the 40% decline in the subcategory of Benevolences.

For the NAE-affiliated denominations, per member giving as a percentage of income declined 32% from the 1968 base in Congregational Finances, and 34% in Benevolences.

In 1968, the NCC-member denominations were giving 3.35% of their incomes to their churches. Of that, 2.71% went to Congregational Finances. In 1985, of the 2.99% of income donated to these communions, 2.52% went to Congregational Finances. This represented a percent change from the 1968 base in the portion of income going to Congregational Finances of -7%. In contrast, per member contributions as a percent of income to Benevolences among these same NCC-affiliated denominations had declined from 0.64% in 1968 to 0.47% in 1985, representing a percent change of -27% from the 1968 base in the portion of income donated to Benevolences.

In 1994, the 2.93% of income donated by the NCC-affiliated members to their churches was divided between Congregational Finances and Benevolences at the 2.55% and 0.38% levels, respectively. Although the per member Total Contributions as a percent of income decreased from 2.99% to 2.93% between 1985 and 1994, the amount of income directed to Congregational Finances increased, from 2.52% in 1985 to 2.55% in 1994. The percent change in contributions to Congregational Finances as a percent of income from the 1985 base was an increase of 1%.

The portion of income directed to Benevolences by these NCC-member denominations had declined from 1968 to 1985, and continued to decline from 1985 to 1994. The percent change in contributions to Benevolences as a percent of income had declined from the 1985 base of 0.47% to the 1994 level of 0.38%, a decline of 18% in this nine-year interval. The annual percent change from the 1985 base in giving as a percentage of income to Benevolences indicated a higher rate of decline at -2.04% between 1985 and 1994, compared to the 1968-1985 annual rate of -1.58%.

In 1968, the NAE-affiliated members were giving 6.19% of their incomes to their churches. Of that, 5.03% went to Congregational Finances, while 1.16% went to Benevolences. In 1985, of the 4.95% of income donated to Total Contributions, 3.99% was directed to Congregational Finances. This represented a percent change in the portion of income going to Congregational Finances of -21% from the 1968 base. Per member contributions to Benevolences among these NAE-member denominations declined from 1.16% in 1968 to 0.96% in 1985, representing a percent change of -17% from the 1968 base in the portion of income donated to Benevolences.

In 1994, the 4.16% of income donated by the NAE-member denominations to their churches was divided between Congregational Finances and Benevolences at the 3.40% and 0.76% levels, respectively. The percent change between 1985 and 1994 in contributions to Congregational Finances as a percent of income, from the 1985 base, was a decline of 15%. In contrast, the percent change in contributions to Benevolences as a percent of income was a decline of 21% in the same nine-year interval. The annual rate in the percent change in giving as a percentage of income to Benevolences, from the 1985 base, accelerated to -2.36% percent between 1985 and 1994, compared to the 1968-1985 rate of -0.98%.

Table 11 presents the 1968-1994 percent change in per member giving as a percentage of income to Total Contributions, Congregational Finances and Benevolences in both the NAE- and NCC-affiliated communions.

Table 11:   Percent Change in Per Member Giving as a Percentage of Income in Eight NAE and Eight NCC Denominations, 1968 to 1994

	NAE Denominations				NCC Denominations			
Year	Number of Denom. Analyzed	Total Contrib.	Cong. Finances	Benevol.	Number of Denom. Analyzed	Total Contrib.	Cong. Finances	Benevol.
1968	8	6.19%	5.03%	1.16%	8	3.35%	2.71%	0.64%
1994	8	4.16%	3.40%	0.76%	8	2.93%	2.55%	0.38%
% Chng, '68-'94 from '68 Base	8	-33%	-32%	-34%	8	-13%	-6%	-40%

Details in the above table may not compute to the numbers shown due to rounding.

Figure 4 presents data for giving as a percentage of income to Total Contributions, Congregational Finances and Benevolences for both the NAE and NCC denominations in graphic form for the years 1968, 1985 and 1994.

Per Member Giving in Constant 1987 Dollars. The NAE-affiliated group level of per member support to Total Contributions in constant 1987 dollars was $608.07 in 1968. This increased to $651.32 in 1985, and declined by 1994 to $629.77.

For the NAE-affiliated denominations, per member contributions in constant 1987 dollars to both subcategories of Congregational Finances and Benevolences followed the same pattern as Total Contributions, increasing between 1968 and 1985, and decreasing between 1985 and 1994.

The NCC-affiliated group experienced an increase in constant dollar per member Total Contributions between 1968 and 1994. The 1968 NCC level of per member support

Figure 4:   Per Member Giving as a Percentage of Income to Total Contributions, Congregational Finances and Benevolences, Eight NAE and Eight NCC Denominations, 1968, 1985 and 1994

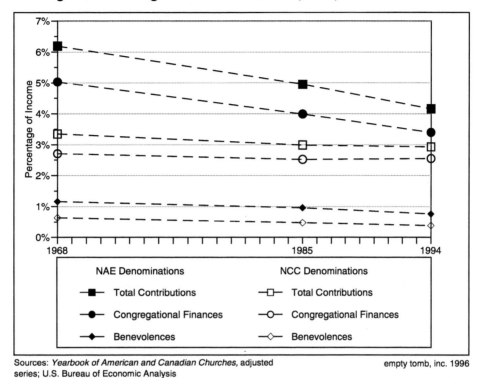

Sources: *Yearbook of American and Canadian Churches,* adjusted
series; U.S. Bureau of Economic Analysis

empty tomb, inc. 1996

in constant 1987 dollars was $329.01. In 1985, this had increased to $392.96, and in 1994 the figure was $443.39.

The NCC-member denominations experienced an increase in constant dollar per member donations to Congregational Finances in both 1985 and 1994 as well. However, gifts to Benevolences declined in both years from the previous level in constant 1987 dollars.

As a portion of Total Contributions, the NAE-member denominations directed 19% of their per member gifts to Benevolences in 1968, 19% in 1985 and 18% in 1994. The NCC-member denominations directed 19% of their per member gifts to Benevolences in 1968, 16% in 1985 and 13% in 1994.

Table 12 below presents the levels of per member giving to Total Contributions, Congregational Finances and Benevolences, in constant 1987 dollars, and the percentage of Total Contributions which went to Benevolences in 1968, 1985 and 1994, for both sets of denominations. In addition, the percent change from the 1968 base in per member constant 1987 dollar contributions from 1968 to 1994 is noted.

Figure 5 presents the data for per member contributions in constant 1987 dollars in graphic form for the years 1968, 1985 and 1994.

Aggregate Dollar Donations. A decrease from 1968 to 1994 in per member giving as a percentage of income to all categories among the NAE-member and NCC-member denominations in this analysis suggests that the decline in giving patterns is evident among

31

Table 12: **Per Member Giving in Eight NAE and Eight NCC Denominations, 1968, 1985 and 1994, Constant 1987 Dollars**

Year	NAE Denominations					NCC Denominations				
	Number of Denom. Analyzed	Total Contrib.	Cong. Finances	Benevol.	Benevol. as % of Total Contrib.	Number of Denom. Analyzed	Total Contrib.	Cong. Finances	Benevol.	Benevol. as % of Total Contrib.
1968	8	$608.07	$494.34	$113.73	19%	8	$329.01	$266.42	$62.59	19%
1985	8	$651.32	$524.56	$126.76	19%	8	$392.96	$331.75	$61.21	16%
1994	8	$629.77	$514.84	$114.92	18%	8	$443.39	$385.86	$57.53	13%
% Chg., '68-'94 from '68 Base		3.57%	4.15%	1.05%			34.77%	44.83%	-8.08%	

Details in the above table may not compute to the numbers shown due to rounding.

church members, and the church structures they support, across the theological spectrum. Whatever factors are contributing to this decline, they are not limited to one specific part of the church.

Among the NCC-member churches, per member giving as a percentage of income declined from 1968 to 1994. In terms of per member constant 1987 dollar gifts, the data indicates an increase to Total Contributions and Congregational Finances, but a decline in per member gifts to Benevolences. A number of the NCC-affiliated denominations have

Figure 5: **Per Member Giving to Total Contributions, Congregational Finances and Benevolences in Eight NAE and Eight NCC Member Denominations, 1968, 1985 and 1994, Constant 1987 Dollars**

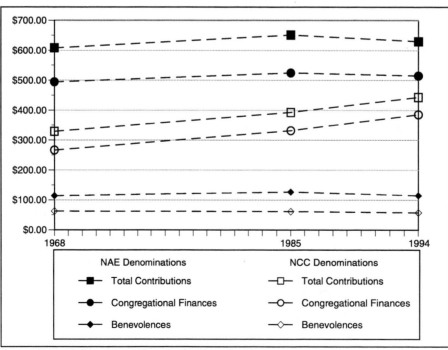

Sources: *Yearbook of American and Canadian Churches,* adjusted series; U.S. Bureau of Economic Analysis

empty tomb, inc. 1996

experienced a decline in income resulting in staff cutbacks at the national, and in some cases regional, levels.

However, while the mainline denominations have conducted highly publicized downsizing during the 1968-1994 period, a similar pattern was not evident among the evangelical communions during these same years. A contributing factor to this difference is the growth in members that the evangelical denominations experienced, in contrast to the membership decline reported by the mainline denominations.

The difference between the two groupings of denominations is that, while both decreased in per member giving to Benevolences as a percentage of income, the NAE-member denominations grew in membership, and the NCC-member denominations declined in membership. In the NAE-affiliated communions, while members were giving a smaller percentage of income, and just one percent more per member in constant dollars to Benevolences in 1994 than in 1968, the aggregate total dollars available increased, as indicated in Table 13 below. For the NCC-affiliated communions, a decline in per member giving as a percentage of income, as well as in constant 1987 dollars to Benevolences, was coupled with a decrease in membership. Thus, for the NCC-affiliated communions, there was a decrease in constant dollars in aggregate Benevolences between 1968 and 1994, as presented in Table 14 below.

Table 13 considers data for the eight NAE-member denominations included in this study for which data was available for both 1968 and 1994. Membership in these eight NAE-member denominations increased 52% from 1968-1994. Table 12 above indicates that per member gifts to Benevolences increased $1.20 (rounded) in constant 1987 dollars from 1968-1994. However, more people giving about the same level of donations still produced a larger total dollar amount.

In current dollars, there were more dollars in each of the three categories of Total Contributions, Congregational Finances and Benevolences in 1994 than in 1968 for the NAE-member denominations.

The same can be said for the three aggregate categories when inflation was factored out by converting the current dollars to constant 1987 dollars. These denominations have been compensated for a relatively static level of contribution per member by the increase in total membership. As long as these denominations continue to grow in membership and maintain constant levels of giving, their programs may not be affected in the immediate future

Table 13:   Aggregate Giving, Eight NAE Denominations, 1968 and 1994, in Current and Constant 1987 Dollars

Year	# Den. Analyzed	Membership	Current Dollars			Constant 1987 Dollars		
			Total Contributions	Cong. Finances	Benevol.	Total Contributions	Cong. Finances	Benevol
1968	8	535,522	$101,923,579	$82,861,129	$19,062,450	$325,634,438	$264,732,042	$60,902,396
1994	8	811,572	$649,609,731	$531,064,936	$118,544,795	$511,101,283	$417,832,365	$93,268,918
% Chg		52%	537%	541%	522%	57%	58%	53%

Details in the above table may not compute to the numbers shown due to rounding.

Table 14: **Aggregate Giving, Eight NCC Denominations, 1968 and 1994, in Current and Constant 1987 Dollars**

Year	# Den. Analyzed	Membership	Current Dollars			Constant 1987 Dollars		
			Total Contributions	Cong. Finances	Benevol	Total Contributions	Cong. Finances	Benevol
1968	8	12,876,821	$1,326,045,714	$1,073,798,710	$252,247,004	$4,236,567,776	$3,430,666,805	$805,900,971
1994	8	9,703,611	$5,468,442,821	$4,758,904,680	$709,538,141	$4,302,472,715	$3,744,220,834	$558,251,881
% Chg		-25%	312%	343%	181%	2%	9%	-31%

Details in the above table may not compute to the numbers shown due to rounding.

in the same way some of the mainline Protestant communions have been impacted by a combination of declining giving and membership.

Table 14 above considers aggregate data for the eight NCC-member denominations for which both 1968 and 1994 data was available. The NCC-related denominations also experienced an increase in current dollars in each of the three categories of Total Contributions, Congregational Finances and Benevolences, even with a posted decline in membership.

However, the constant 1987 dollar figures account for the acknowledged financial difficulties in many of these communions, particularly in the category of Benevolences. The decline in membership affected the total income received by this group of denominations. Between 1968 and 1994, while the NCC-related communions experienced an increase of 35% in per member giving to Total Contributions in constant 1987 dollars—from $329.01 in 1968 to $443.39 in 1994—aggregate Total Contributions in 1994 to these eight denominations were only 2% larger in constant 1987 dollars in 1994 than in 1968.

In regard to the two categories of Congregational Finances and Benevolences, Congregational Finances absorbed the increased giving. The 31% decline in aggregated Benevolences receipts in constant 1987 dollars between 1968 and 1994 provides insight into the basis for any cutbacks at the denominational level.

Summary. An analysis of giving as a percentage of income found a negative trend in church member giving across the theological spectrum between 1968 and 1994. Denominations affiliated with both the NAE and the NCC were receiving a smaller portion of income on a per member basis.

On one hand, the NAE-member denominations received a higher portion of income on a per member basis than did the NCC-member denominations throughout this period. On the other hand, between 1968 and 1985, the NAE-member denominations experienced a higher rate of decrease in average annual percent change in giving as a percentage of income from the 1968 base in the categories of Total Contributions and Congregational Finances than did the NCC-member denominations. In the category of Benevolences, between 1968 and 1985, the NCC-member denominations had a higher rate of decrease in average annual percent change in giving as a percentage of income from the 1968 base than did the NAE-member denominations.

Between 1985 and 1994, the NAE-member denominations experienced a higher rate of decrease in average annual percent change in per member giving as a percentage of income from the 1985 base than did the NCC-member denominations in each of the three categories of Total Contributions, Congregational Finances and Benevolences. Further, in the category of Congregational Finances, the NCC-member denominations increased slightly from 1985 to 1994.

In both the NAE-member and NCC-member denominations, the rate of decrease in per member giving as a percentage of income to Benevolences quickened during the 1985-1994 period compared to the 1968-1985 period.

After inflation was factored out by converting the data to constant 1987 dollars, both the NAE-affiliated and the NCC-affiliated denominations received more dollars per member for the categories of Total Contributions and Congregational Finances in 1994 than in 1968. In the Benevolences category, the NAE-affiliated denominations received $1.20 more per member in constant 1987 dollars, an increase of 1.05% between 1968 and 1994. The NCC-affiliated denominations received $5.06 less per member in constant 1987 dollars, a decline of 8%.

Because the NAE-affiliated denominations were growing in membership during the 1968-1994 period, aggregate income to these denominations increased, even though 1994 per member constant dollar giving to Benevolences was close to the 1968 level. A decline in per member giving in constant 1987 dollars to Benevolences in the NCC-affiliated denominations coincided with a decline in membership in those denominations. The result was a decrease in aggregate Benevolences for the NCC-member denominations between 1968 and 1994.

The generally-held belief that evangelicals were "better givers" than mainline members was correct in that per member giving was higher in the NAE-affiliated denominations both in terms of giving as a percentage of income and constant dollar contributions when compared to NCC-member denominations throughout the 1968 to 1994 period.

However, the rate of decline in per member giving as a percentage of income between 1985 and 1994 was more pronounced among the NAE-affiliated denominations than among the NCC-affiliated denominations.

The negative direction in per member giving as a percentage of income over the 27-year time span under review in both the NAE-affiliated and NCC-affiliated denominations suggested the negative trend in giving patterns is not limited to a particular denomination or a particular portion of the theological spectrum.

4

Church Member Giving
in Eleven Denominations, 1921-1994_____

According to the composite data for 29 Protestant denominations, the portion of income given to the church declined over the last 27 years, from 1968-1994.

How do the giving patterns in this 27-year period compare to church member giving data throughout this century? Was there a time frame during which giving was increasing, or where giving levels were consistently higher than others?

Unfortunately, data is not available for all 29 communions in the composite analysis throughout this century. However, data over an extended period of time is available in the *Yearbook of American and Canadian Churches* series for a group of 11 Protestant communions, or their historical antecedents. The available data has been reported fairly consistently over the time span of 1921 to 1994.[7] The value of the multiyear comparison is that it provides a historical time line over which to observe giving patterns.

This data indicates that the period 1947-1960 produced the highest level of sustained increase in per member giving during the 74-year period of 1921-1994.

Figure 6 contrasts per member giving as a percentage of income for a composite of eleven Protestant denominations, with U.S. disposable personal income in constant 1987 dollars, for the period 1921 through 1994.

Giving as a Percentage of Income. The period under consideration in this section of the report began in 1921. At that point, per member giving as a percentage of income was 2.9%. In current dollars, U.S. per capita disposable (after-tax) personal income was $555, and per member giving was $16. When inflation was factored out by converting both income and giving to constant 1987 dollars, per capita income in 1921 measured $4,188 and per member giving was $122.

---

[7] Data for the period 1965-1967 was not available in a form that could be readily analyzed for the present purposes, and therefore data for these three years was estimated by dividing the change in per member current dollar contributions from 1964 to 1968 by four, the number of years in this interval, and cumulatively adding the result to the base year of 1964 and the succeeding years of 1965 and 1966 to obtain estimates for the years 1965-1967.

Figure 6: **Per Member Giving as a Percentage of Income in 11 Denominations, and U.S. Per Capita Income 1921-1994**

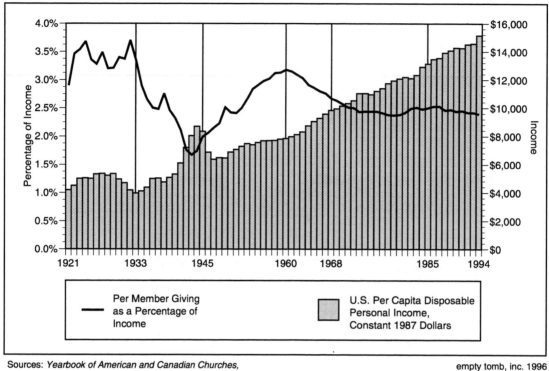

Sources: *Yearbook of American and Canadian Churches,*
adjusted series; U.S. Bureau of Economic Analysis

empty tomb, inc. 1996

The year 1933 was the depth of the Great Depression. Per capita income was at the lowest point it would reach between 1921 and 1994, whether measured in current or constant dollars. Yet per member giving as a percentage of income was 3.3%. Income had decreased by 5% between 1921 and 1933 in constant 1987 dollars, from $4,188 to $3,967. Yet per member giving had increased 9%, from $122 in 1921 to $133 in 1933, in constant 1987 dollars.

During World War II, incomes improved, reaching a high point in 1944, when per capita income measured $8,702 in constant 1987 dollars, a level that would not be surpassed again until 1964. In 1945, the last year of the war, U.S. per capita income was $8,344 in constant 1987 dollars. Giving in constant 1987 dollars was $166 in 1945. Although per member giving increased 25% between 1933 and 1945, per capita income had increased 110%. Giving as a percentage of income therefore declined from the 3.3% level in 1933, to 2.0% in 1945.

The unusually high level of per capita income ended with the war. By 1960, U.S. per capita income was 6% lower in constant 1987 dollars than it had been in 1945, declining from $8,344 in 1945 to $7,850 in 1960. Meanwhile, per member giving in constant 1987 dollars had increased 50%, from $166 in 1945 to $249 in 1960. As a result, giving as a percentage of income reached a postwar high of 3.2% in 1960.

In 1968, giving as a percentage of income had declined to 2.7% for this group of 11 communions. U.S. per capita income increased 25% in constant 1987 dollars between 1960 and 1968, from $7,850 in 1960 to $9,831 in 1968. However, per member giving had only increased 5% in constant 1987 dollars, from the 1960 level of $249 to the 1968 level of $263.

By 1985, per member giving had increased 25% in constant 1987 dollars, from $263 in 1968 to $329 in 1985. U.S. per capita income measured $13,155, an increase of 34% over the 1968 level of $9,831. Giving as a percentage of income measured 2.5% in 1985.

The year 1994 was the latest year for which data was available for the eleven denominations considered in this section. In that year, per member giving as a percentage of income was 2.4%, a slight decline from the 1985 level of 2.5%. Per member giving had increased 10% in constant 1987 dollars, from $329 in 1985 to $362 in 1994. However, U.S. per capita income had increased 15% during this period, from the 1985 level of $13,155 to the 1994 level of $15,148.

Change in Per Member Giving in Constant 1987 Dollars. For this group of 11 communions, per member giving in constant 1987 dollars generally displayed a pattern of alternately increasing for one, two or three years in a row, and then decreasing for one or more years during the 1921-1947 period with one exception. Not surprisingly, per member giving posted declines six years in a row during 1930-1935, which included the worst years of the Great Depression. In 1936, the per member giving pattern of one, two or three years of increases followed by one or two years of decreases in constant 1987 dollars resumed.

Then, from 1947 through 1968,[8] these 11 communions experienced uninterrupted increases in per member giving in constant 1987 dollars for 21 years in a row. Further, the period from 1947 to the year 1960, when giving as a percentage of income reached its postwar peak, posted the highest prolonged annual increase in per member giving in constant dollars during this 1921-1994 73-year interval. During the 1947-1960 13-year interval, per member giving averaged an increase of $8.62 a year. Although giving continued to increase for the next few years from 1960 to 1968, it was at the much slower rate of $1.67 per year.

Per member giving in constant dollars declined annually from 1968 through 1971, followed by three years of increase and one of decline. The next prolonged period of increase was from 1975 through 1994. During this period, giving changed annually by $4.94. This was 43% less per year than the annual rate of change between 1947 and 1960 of $8.62.

By reviewing this data in five-year periods from 1950 to 1994, as presented in Table 15, the time period in which giving began to decline markedly can be identified.

As indicated in Table 15, the period 1950 to 1955 was the period of highest annual increase in per member giving in constant 1987 dollars. However, the period 1955 to 1960 was the period of highest annual increase as a percentage of the annual change in U.S. per capita income. The period 1980 to 1985 produced a higher average per member annual dollar increase than that given in 1955-1960. However, the larger amount of $8.43 represented only 3.92% of the average annual increase in U.S. per capita income, compared to the 10% which the $5.86 represented from 1955 to 1960.

---

[8] Excluding the years 1965 through 1967 for which estimated data is used. See first footnote in this chapter.

Table 15:   **Average Annual Increase in U.S. Per Capita Income and Per Member Giving in 11 Denominations, 1950-1994, Constant 1987 Dollars**

Time Period	U.S. Per Capita Income			Per Member Giving			
	First Year in Period	Last Year in Period	Average Annual Change	First Year in Period	Last Year in Period	Average Annual Change	Giv. Incr. as % of Income Increase
1950-1955	$6,879	$7,558	$135.73	$166.68	$220.11	$10.69	7.87%
1955-1960	$7,558	$7,850	$58.47	$220.11	$249.43	$5.86	10.03%
1960-1964	$7,850	$8,742	$222.83	$249.43	$254.21	$1.19	0.54%
1964-1970	$8,742	$10,147	$234.21	$254.21	$260.71	$1.08	0.46%
1970-1975	$10,147	$10,965	$163.61	$260.71	$268.02	$1.46	0.89%
1975-1980	$10,965	$12,079	$222.77	$268.02	$287.31	$3.86	1.73%
1980-1985	$12,079	$13,155	$215.14	$287.31	$329.45	$8.43	3.92%
1985-1990	$13,155	$14,278	$224.59	$329.45	$348.23	$3.76	1.67%
1990-1994	$14,278	$15,148	$217.60	$348.23	$361.92	$3.42	1.57%

Details in the above table may not compute to the numbers shown due to rounding.

However, giving declined markedly between 1960 and 1964 in these communions.[9] While income was increasing at an annual rate of $223 in this four-year period, 281% greater than in the 1955-1960 period, the average annual increase in per member contributions in constant 1987 dollars was $1.19, 80% smaller in 1960-1964 than it was in 1955-1960.

The 1960-1964 period predates many of the controversial issues often cited as reasons for declining giving. Also, it was at the end of the 1960-1964 period when membership began to decrease in mainline denominations, ten of which are included in this group. Therefore, additional exploration of that period of time might be merited.

Increases in per member giving were consistently low from 1960-1975. The annual rate of increase was $1.19 per year from 1960 to 1964, $1.08 from 1964 to 1970, and $1.46 from 1970 to 1975. Throughout the 1960 to 1975 period, the increase in dollars given represented less than one percent of the average annual increase in per capita income.

In the 1975-1980 period, the average annual increase in giving increased to $3.86, representing 1.73% of the average annual increase in per capita income.

From 1980 to 1985, the average annual increase in giving rose to $8.43. This amount of $8.43—representing 3.92% of the average annual increase in income during the 1980-1985 period—was the second highest average annual rate of increase in terms of per member giving in constant dollars during the 1950 to 1994 period. As a portion of the increase in per capita income, the 3.92% of the 1980 to 1985 period was the third largest annual rate of increase in the 1950 to 1994 period.

The annual average increase in giving from 1985 to 1990 fell below that of both the 1975 to 1980 and 1980 to 1985 periods, and decreased again in the four-year period from 1990 to 1994. The rate decreased both in terms of increase in per member giving in constant dollars and as a portion of the average annual income increase.

---

[9] See the first footnote in this chapter for an explanation of the selection of 1960-1964 and 1964-1970, rather than 1960-1965 and 1965-1970

Giving in 1994 Compared to 1921 and 1933. By 1994, U.S. per capita disposable (after-tax) personal income had increased 262%, in constant 1987 dollars, since 1921, and 282% since 1933—the depth of the Great Depression.

Meanwhile, per member giving in constant 1987 dollars in 1994 had increased 198% since 1921, and 173% since the depth of the Great Depression.

As a result, per member giving as a percentage of income was lower in 1994 than in either 1921 or 1933. In 1921, per member giving as a percentage of income was 2.9%. In 1933, it was 3.3%. In 1994, per member giving as a percentage of income was 2.4% for a composite of the eleven denominations considered in this section. Thus, the percent change in the per member portion of income donated to the church had declined by 18% from the 1921 base, from 2.9% in 1921 to 2.4% in 1994.

Summary. During the period from 1947 through 1960, the average annual increase in per member giving in constant 1987 dollars was $8.62, the highest consistent rate of increase in the 1921 to 1994 period. Giving continued to increase on an annual basis from 1960-1968, although at a slower rate than during 1947-1960. Per member giving in constant 1987 dollars also increased annually for 19 years from 1975 through 1994, although the average annual increase was lower from 1975-1994 than in the years just after World War II, from 1947-1960.

Per member giving in constant 1987 dollars was increasing at an annual rate of $10.69 in 1950-1955, representing 8% of the annual increase in U.S. per capita disposable personal income of $136. In 1955-1960 the rate of annual increase in giving declined to $5.86. However, this rate of increase represented 10% of the annual increase in U.S. per capita income of $58.

A marked decline in the portion of the increase in constant dollar income directed to the church was noted from 1960-1975, with the years 1964 to 1970 displaying the smallest average annual increase in the 1950-1994 period.

Giving increased in both the 1975-1980 and 1980-1985 periods, and declined in both the 1985-1990 and 1990-1994 periods, although the annual increase in giving was higher than in the 1960-1975 period during these last two sets of years.

Giving was higher as a portion of income in both 1921 and 1933 than in 1994.

Appendix A contains a listing of the denominations contained in this analysis.

5

Church Member Giving and Membership Trends Based on 1968-1994 Data

The consequences of the church member patterns discussed in previous chapters have already been felt by some of the denominations included in the analyses. There have been efforts to economize, and in some cases downsize, operations. Various strategies from new church starts to innovative stewardship techniques have been applied in an attempt to alter giving and membership levels.

In addition to immediate consequences, what implications will these patterns have if they continue in an uninterrupted fashion? Various segments of society use such analysis to develop strategies or plot their course. Government projects global warming rates, the economic parity of women, and population growth to inform current policies.

In the example of global warming, the Intergovernmental Panel on Climate Change forecast a temperature increase by the year 2100. The trend was so pronounced that even countries likely to be adversely affected by the policies that will be designed to prevent this warming were part of the unanimous conclusion.[10]

The purpose of such forecasts is to plot the consequences of current behavior in an attempt to evaluate whether the results are in keeping with the idea of a satisfactory future. If the outcome of such analysis is not acceptable, logic suggests that current patterns should be altered in a way that will effect an alternative scenario.

Such trend analysis may also be useful in considering what data from the past three decades suggests the future will look like if current patterns continue in an uninterrupted fashion.

The Meaning of Trends. Trend projections using linear regression should always be evaluated knowing that such projections indicate—rather than dictate—future directions. For example, in the present church member giving analysis, the data can be used to develop giving trends that suggest what giving will look like in the next two centuries. These trends only indicate the present general direction of giving. Various factors—such as intentional education efforts by congregations and/or denominations, or spiritual renewal, or a decided loss of commitment to the church—could change giving patterns in unforeseen ways, either

---

[10] Sharon Begley, "He's Not Full of Hot Air," *Newsweek*, January 22, 1996, 25.

positively or negatively. Trends, therefore, are based on the assumption that current conditions will remain constant. The trends point out the future of giving, if patterns continue without interruption. With those considerations in mind, it is of value to explore what implications present data patterns have for the future.

After talking with numerous denominational officials who were making painful decisions about which programs to cut, in light of decreased Benevolences dollars being received, it seemed useful to see where the present patterns of giving might lead if effective means were not found to alter present behavior. Were current patterns likely to prove a temporary setback, or did the data suggest longer-term implications?

The Trend in Church Giving. The earlier sections of this report indicate that per member giving as a percentage of income has been decreasing over a 27-year period. Further, contributions to the category of Benevolences have been declining proportionately faster than those to Congregational Finances between 1968 and 1994. In addition, the per member contribution for Benevolences in constant dollars was lower in 1994 than it was in 1968.

The data for the composite denominations analyzed for 1968 through 1994 has been projected in *The State of Church Giving* series, beginning with the edition that included 1991 data.[11] The most recent projection includes data from 1968 through 1994.

Trends in Benevolences. Of the two subcategories within Total Contributions, that is, Congregational Finances and Benevolences, the more pronounced negative trend occurred in Benevolences. Between 1968 and 1994, per member contributions to Benevolences as a percentage of income decreased from 0.66% in 1968 to 0.42% in 1994, a percent change in giving as a percentage of income of -37% from the 1968 base. In contrast, the percent change in giving as a percentage of income to Congregational Finances declined 17% from the 1968 base, from 2.48% in 1968 to 2.06% in 1994.

When the data for giving as a percentage of income to Benevolences for the 27-year period of 1968 through 1994 was projected using the standard statistical technique of linear regression, per member giving to the category of Benevolences reached 0% of income in the year A.D. 2048.[12] In that year, those categories of expenditures within the definition of Benevolences, including denominational structures, would be receiving no support from per member giving to Total Contributions if current patterns hold constant.

This finding indicates the decline in giving as a percentage of income to Benevolences had slightly accelerated from the previous year. In a previous report, when the Benevolences data for 1968 through 1993 was analyzed using linear regression, per member giving to the category of Benevolences reached 0% of income again in the year A.D. 2049.

---

[11] John Ronsvalle and Sylvia Ronsvalle, *The State of Church Giving through 1991* (Champaign, IL: empty tomb, inc., 1993), and Ronsvalle and Ronsvalle, *The State of Church Giving through 1992* (Champaign, IL: empty tomb, inc., 1994). The edition with data through 1991 provides a discussion of the choice to use giving as a percentage of income as a basis for considering where present giving patterns might go in the future.

[12] The value for the correlation coefficient, or r_{XY}, for the Benevolences data is -.98. The strength of the linear relationship in the present set of data, that is, the proportion of variance accounted for by linear regression, is represented by the coefficient of determination, or r^2_{XY}, of .95 for Benevolences. The Benevolences F-observed value of 501.82 is substantially greater than the F-critical value of 7.77 for 1 and 25 degrees of freedom for a single-tailed test with an Alpha value of 0.01. Therefore, the regression equation is useful at the level suggested by the r^2_{XY} figure in predicting giving as a percentage of income.

With the additional data for 1994 moving the date to 2048, the data suggests the earlier observed trend is continuing.

The Trend in Congregational Finances. The church giving data contained in this report indicated that, while there was a less pronounced trend in the level of Congregational Finances, giving as a percentage of income also declined between 1968 and 1994. Using linear regression based on the data for the 27 years in that time period, the trend suggests that per member giving as a percentage of income would reach 0% in the year A.D. 2199 for Congregational Finances.[13] The previous analysis for 1968-1993 data placed the year at 2203.

Figure 7 illustrates the projected trends for both Benevolences and Congregational Finances as a percentage of income.

Figure 7:   Projected Trends for Giving as a Percentage of Income to Congregational Finances and Benevolences, Data for 1968-1994

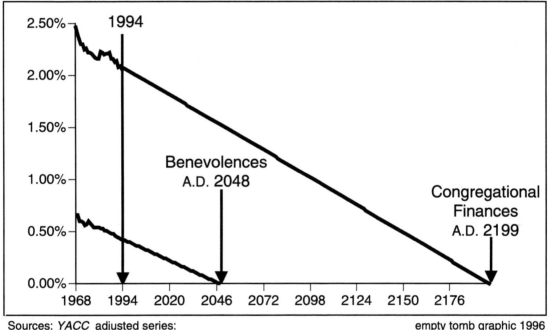

Sources: *YACC* adjusted series: empty tomb graphic 1996
U.S. Bureau of Economic Analysis

Trends in Church Membership as a Percentage of U.S. Population.[14] In *The State of Church Giving through 1993,* one chapter considers a "Unified Theory of Giving and

---

[13] The value for the correlation coefficient, or r_{XY}, for the Congregational Finances data is -.86. The strength of the linear relationship in the present set of data, that is, the proportion of variance accounted for by linear regression, is represented by the coefficient of determination, or r^2_{XY}, of .75 for Congregational Finances. The Congregational Finances F-observed value of 73.04 is substantially greater than the F-critical value of 7.77 for 1 and 25 degrees of freedom for a single-tailed test with an Alpha value of 0.01. Therefore, the regression equation is useful at the level suggested by the r^2_{XY} figure in predicting giving as a percentage of income.

[14] The denominations analyzed in this section include the composite of 29 communions analyzed elsewhere in this report. The data for 29 communions is supplemented by the data of 9 denominations included in an analysis of church membership and U.S. population by Roozen and Hadaway in David A. Roozen and Kirk C. Hadaway, eds., *Church and Denominational Growth* (Nashville: Abingdon Press, 1993), 393-395.

Membership." The hypothesis explored in that discussion is that there is a relationship between declines in church member giving and patterns in membership. One proposal considered in that chapter is that a denomination which is able to involve its members in a larger vision as evidenced in giving patterns will also be attracting additional members.

In the present edition, discussion will be limited to patterns and trends in membership as a percentage of U.S. population.

Membership in the Composite 29 Denominations. The earlier chapters discuss the patterns in church member giving in a composite of 29 denominations. How do membership patterns for this group of denominations fare in addition to their giving patterns?

This group of denominations which span the theological spectrum included 28,163,801 Full or Confirmed Members in 1968. By 1994, these communions included 30,576,453 members, an increase of 9%. However, during the same 27-year period, U.S. population had increased from 200,745,000 to 260,681,000, an increase of 30%. Therefore, while this grouping represented 14% of the U.S. population in 1968, it included 12% in 1994. Figure 8 presents per member giving as a percentage of income as well as membership as a percentage of U.S. population for these 29 denominations.

Figure 8:   Giving as a Percentage of Income and Membership as a Percentage of U.S. Population, 29 Denominations, 1968-1994

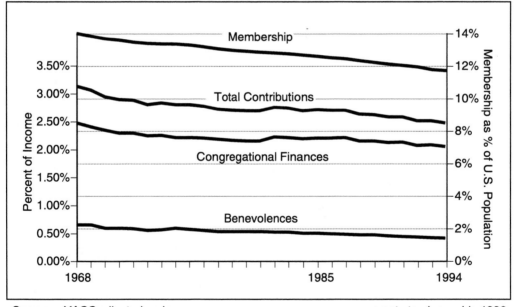

Sources: *YACC* adjusted series;   empty tomb graphic 1996
U.S. Bureau of Economic Analysis

Membership in Ten Mainline Denominations. The declining membership trends have been noticed most markedly in the mainline Protestant communions. A group of ten mainline Protestant denominations indicate this group of communions decreased as a percentage of U.S. population by 40% between 1968 and 1994. In 1968, this group included 26,389,216, or 13.1% of U. S. population. In 1994, the group included 20,676,287, or 7.9% of U.S. population.

Linear regression was used to project a trend based on the 1968-1994 membership data for these ten mainline Protestant communions, all of which were affiliated with the

National Council of the Churches of Christ in the U.S.A.[15] As shown in Figure 9, these communions would constitute 0% of the U.S. population in the year A.D. 2036, or 42 years from the last year of available data, if current patterns remain the same.[16]

Figure 9:   Trend in Membership as a Percent of U.S. Population, Ten Mainline Protestant Denominations, Data for 1968-1994

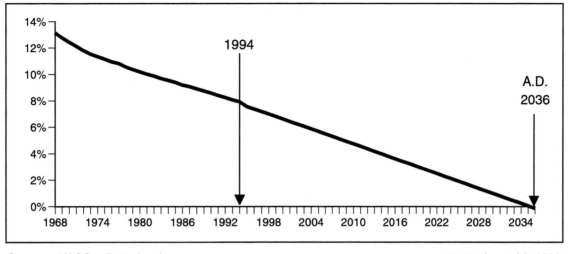

Sources: *YACC* adjusted series: empty tomb graphic 1996
U.S. Bureau of Economic Analysis

Membership in an Expanded Set of Communions. Of course, these ten denominations represent only one segment of the body of Christ. Protestant denominations have varying membership trends. In the composite of 29 Protestant communions considered in earlier chapters of this report, some of the evangelical and conservative denominations were growing in membership even while mainline denominations were declining. In addition, membership data for the period 1968-1994 is available for several additional Protestant communions as well, bringing the number of Protestant denominations with available data to 36. When one considers whether the Protestant church in the U.S. may be reduced to remnant status at some point in the future, a larger grouping of denominations would provide additional insight by expanding the base of information.

In 1968, these 36 Protestant denominations represented 42,629,775 members, and in 1994, a total of 43,541,386, an increase of 2%. Meanwhile, the overall population in the U.S. had been growing at a faster rate than the membership changes posted by these denominations. As a result, these communions were 21% of the U.S. population in 1968, and 17% in 1994. The trend for the rate of growth in the denominations and growth in U.S. population

---

[15] These ten denominations include 8 of the communions in the composite of 29 denominations as well as data for The Episcopal Church and The United Methodist Church is included. The Friends United Meeting data is not considered in the membership projections, since data was not available after 1990 for that communion.

[16] The value for the correlation coefficient, or r_{XY}, for the Full or Confirmed Membership data is -.99. The strength of the linear relationship in the present set of data, that is, the proportion of variance accounted for by linear regression, is represented by the coefficient of determination, or r^2_{XY}, of .99 for Membership. The Membership F-observed value of 1800.53 is substantially greater than the F-critical value of 7.77 for 1 and 25 degrees of freedom for a single-tailed test with an Alpha value of 0.01. Therefore, the regression equation is useful at the level suggested by the r^2_{XY} figure in predicting membership.

over the past 27 years suggests that these groups would constitute 0% of the U.S. population in the year A.D. 2100, or roughly four times the span from 1968 to 1994, once again if present patterns remain constant. This information is presented in Figure 10.[17]

Figure 10:   Trend in Membership as a Percent of U.S. Population, 10 Mainline Protestant and 26 Other Protestant Denominations, Data for 1968-1994

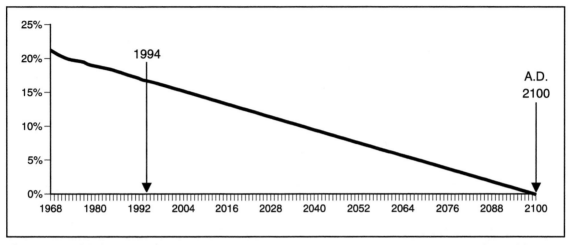

Sources: *YACC* adjusted series: empty tomb graphic 1996
U.S. Bureau of Economic Analysis

Of course, the picture would be incomplete without the Roman Catholic Church. Adding in this membership data with that of the 36 Protestant communions considered above results in this combination of Catholic and Protestant communions including 90,098,108 members in 1968. With the U.S. population at 200,745,000, these Christians were 45% of the U.S. population. By 1994, the group had grown to 103,731,991 members. However, the U.S. population had grown to 260,681,000. Now these Christians were 40% of the American population.

If the rate of membership growth of the past 27 years were to hold steady in the future for these 37 Christian communions, and the same were true for growth in U.S. population, then these communions would represent 0% of the U.S. population in the year A.D. 2220.

While two centuries may seem like a long time from the present discussion, concern may be expressed about the fact that a process of marginalization of the church in American society would be occurring throughout this period, if these trends hold true. The fact that the 36 Protestant denominations, when combined with the Roman Catholic Church data, constituted 45% of the U.S. population in 1968 and 40% in 1994 suggests that there is an overall decrease in membership in the U.S. in the historically Christian church.

---

[17] The value for the correlation coefficient, or r_{XY}, for the Full or Confirmed Membership data is -1.00. The strength of the linear relationship in the present set of data, that is, the proportion of variance accounted for by linear regression, is represented by the coefficient of determination, or r^2_{XY}, of .99 for Membership. The Membership F-observed value of 2923.80 is substantially greater than the F-critical value of 7.77 for 1 and 25 degrees of freedom for a single-tailed test with an Alpha value of 0.01. Therefore, the regression equation is useful at the level suggested by the r^2_{XY} figure in predicting membership.

The Response to the Trends. As in other sectors, trend lines in church giving and membership are designed to provide another source of information. Planning, evaluation and creative thinking are some of the types of constructive responses which can be made in light of projections. The information on church member giving and membership trends is offered as a possible planning tool.[18] The trend lines are not considered to be dictating what must happen, but rather as providing important indicators of what might happen if present conditions continue in an uninterrupted fashion. The results of the analysis may be useful as additional input to inform decisions by church leaders in the present.

The data reflects trends that raise important implications for the future. One might liken the projection to a symptom of illness. If a person is running a temperature of 104°, the choice would be to call the doctor or hope the fever runs its course. In either case, the body is communicating that there is a condition present which requires attention. Trends in church giving and membership, if used wisely, may be of assistance in addressing conditions present in the body of Christ in the U.S.

---

[18] For additional discussion of the implications of the trends, see Ronsvalle and Ronsvalle, *The State of Church Giving through 1991*, pp. 61-67.

6

Retrospective of *The State of Church Giving* Series_____

The State of Church Giving through 1994 is the seventh in a series of reports that considers patterns in church member giving patterns. The earlier chapters in this edition update the analyses that appear in each edition of the series. In addition, each report in the series has presented one or more particular issues for discussion and consideration. The following summaries describe previous special focus topics that were considered in earlier editions in the series. At the end of the chapter, information is provided if the reader would like to obtain the complete text of a particular chapter that is summarized below.

The summaries that follow are largely taken from a paper that was presented by the authors as part of a Religious Research Association (RRA) panel at the combined annual meeting with the Society for the Scientific Study of Religion held November 8-10, 1996 in Nashville, Tennessee.

The final section of this chapter, taken from the RRA paper, also considers general approaches to church-related research.

"An Exploration of Roman Catholic Giving Patterns"
(from *The State of Church Giving through 1993*)

Church member giving data for the Roman Catholic Church has not been published in the *Yearbook of American and Canadian Churches* (*YACC*) or other regular series since the mid-1930s, when the U.S. Census stopped collecting church data. Therefore, giving patterns for Catholics have relied heavily on survey results. Those results suggest that per member giving to the church among Catholics is lower than that for Protestants. Denominational data and other published sources of church member financial data helped to develop a model for Catholic giving patterns.

A first step in exploring this idea was to develop a model with High, Medium and Low levels of data. Three factors common to any congregation were considered: Clergy compensation; Parishioner-to-Clergy Ratio; and Worship Services per Building. Data on clergy compensation was available in a 1992 study;[19] membership and clergy numbers were

---

[19] Todd Van Campen, ed., *1992 Church Compensation Report: Nationwide Comparison of Pay and Benefits for Full- and Part-Time Church Employees* (Carol Stream, IL: Christianity Today, Inc., 1991), 41, 83, 126. Total Compensation is defined as "base salary plus benefits including housing, compensation, pension/retirement, taxes and insurance" (Van Campen, page 5).

available from both the *Yearbook of American and Canadian Churches* as well as the *Official Catholic Directory*; and the number of worship services per building was estimated.

Using these sources the data in the High level of the model suggested that the average Catholic Total Compensation for priests was $19,645 in 1991. For Protestant clergy, it was $37,011. The Parishioner-to-Priest Ratio was 1,699 for Catholics, and for Protestants, the Parishioner-to-Clergy Ratio was 347. The High model also used an estimate of five Masses per building for Catholics and one service for Protestants. An estimate for total Catholic giving was obtained from the work of Joseph Claude Harris, who estimated that giving was $5.479 billion to Sunday collections in 1991.[20]

The model considered what would happen if Catholic clergy compensation used a Protestant scale; if the parishioner-to-clergy ratio were at the Protestant level; and capital costs were increased in conjunction with attaining a Protestant norm of one worship service per building (see figure 11). When these factors were accounted for, it was determined that

Figure 11: Comparative Catholic and Protestant Parish Cost Estimates

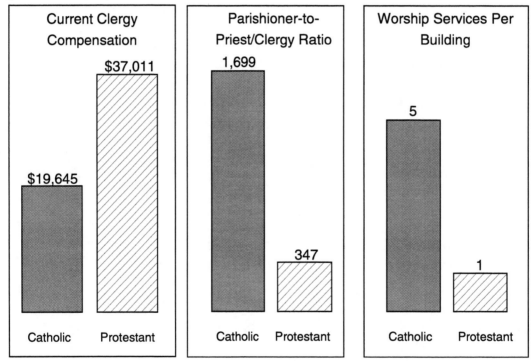

Sources: empty tomb, inc. analysis; *1992 Compensation Report*;   empty tomb graphic 1995
    An Estimate of Catholic Household Contributions; *YACC* series

Catholics would have to give about $319 on average to support the basic operations of the congregation in a manner similar to that in which Protestants operate their congregations. Were that the case, Catholics would be giving on a par with members of the two largest

---

[20] Joseph Claude Harris, *An Estimate of Catholic Household Contributions to the Sunday Offertory Collection During 1991* (Washington, DC: Life Cycle Center of the Catholic University of America, December 1992), 99. While the Sunday collection does not incorporate all parish income and income is not necessarily the same as expenses, this figure is sufficient for the present first approximation estimate purposes.

Protestant communions in the U.S., The United Methodist Church and the Southern Baptist Convention. This preliminary model does not take other income such as diocesan appeals into account; thus the figures on current giving would be increased due to that factor as well.

According to this hypothesis, the current lower level of giving observed among Catholics may be due to an efficiency in the way that Catholic parishes are organized, and the lower support level needed from Catholic members to maintain that organization.

"A Unified Theory of Giving and Membership" (from *The State of Church Giving through 1993*)

This chapter explores the relationship between declines in giving and membership trends. Noting that 30 years of research has not reversed membership declines in mainline Protestant churches, and that membership growth as a percentage of population is leveling off or declining among a number of conservative and evangelical denominations, it is suggested that a new approach may prove fruitful in exploring the issues involved in these patterns.

The introduction to the chapter reads in part:

Traditional studies have not been able to diagnose the dynamics affecting church membership in such a way that concerned people have been able to reverse the declining trends. Therefore, a different approach may be needed. A unified theory of giving and membership may prove productive.

One advantage of connecting the two factors of giving and membership more directly than they have been in the past is that dynamics affecting giving can also be evaluated for their effect on membership trends as well. For example, it may be obvious to consider the effect of the advent of easy credit in the early 1960s on church giving patterns. However, would easy credit affect membership? If the relationship between giving and membership were to be explored, then such issues would be evaluated in a broader context.

Based on this approach, a theory includes the following ideas. Beginning in the 1950s, to the degree that the church did not engage the topic of money in a way that translated into individual behavior patterns, people, including church members, became preoccupied with consumerist-related activities as a function of their increasing affluence. As a result, their giving as a percentage of income declined over time. As the church represented a smaller portion of their total financial commitment, and other activities and possessions came to represent a larger portion, their membership lapsed.

Within this theory, then, the amount of giving becomes an important indicator not only of the level of commitment to one's church, as has been discussed in previous chapters of this report. In addition, the church member's giving—more specifically as a percentage of income, representing available resources—also serves as an indicator of the strength of the barrier between the church member and the influence of the surrounding culture.

Following are two areas considered in the chapter.

Per Member Giving in Mainline Protestant Denominations. A commonly-held assumption is that mainline Protestant denominations have experienced a decrease in income because affiliated congregations have withheld funds due to disagreement with denominational policies. D. Scott Cormode, in a study of the Presbyterian church concluded that such displeasure could not explain the decrease in income.[21] A similar conclusion was reached by Kenneth W. Innskeep about the Evangelical Lutheran Church in America.[22]

The question may be asked, what does additional denominational data suggest? Data for 10 mainline Protestant churches is available on a fairly consistent basis for the years 1953 through 1993. The membership for this group peaked at 26,884,395 in 1964. However, giving as a percentage of income peaked at 3.41% in 1961, three years before membership began a consistent decline, and several years before the controversial issues often credited for dissension within these denominations surfaced in the late 1960s and early 1970s. The data would suggest reasons other than denominational controversy may have contributed to the declines in giving.

Benevolences Giving and Membership. Data for support of giving to denominational overseas ministries is available in the Missions Advanced Research Center (MARC) *Mission Handbook* series.[23] This data, when coupled with membership data from the *YACC* series allowed a consideration of what patterns emerged between support of denominational overseas mission activities and membership patterns. Per member giving to denominational overseas missions and membership for five data years between 1972 and 1991 were compared.

The historical importance of mission suggested that category as one that would clearly garner support within the larger category of Benevolences. The missions giving data from the MARC *Mission Handbook* series included data for five data years over the 1972 to 1991 interval. In two denominations, per member contributions in constant 1987 dollars to denominational overseas ministries activities grew between 1972 and 1991. The Assemblies of God posted a 30% increase in per member contributions to overseas ministries in constant 1987 dollars, and a 95% increase in membership during these years. In the Southern Baptist Convention, the largest Protestant communion in the U.S., per member contributions to overseas missions grew 21%, while membership increased 26%.

Conversely, giving to overseas ministries in the Evangelical Lutheran Church in America declined 43.5% while membership declined 1%, and in the Presbyterian Church (U.S.A.), per member support for overseas missions declined 43% and membership declined 27%. Meanwhile, per member giving to overseas ministries declined 40% between 1972 and 1991 in The United Methodist Church, while membership declined 14% (see figure 12). A supportive culture, especially one that may include geographical boundaries such as the South for Southern Baptists, or the North Central region of the U.S. for Lutherans, may help insulate some church groups against pressures that resulted in decreased membership in other traditions.[24] This hypothesis may account for the decline in mission giving among Lutherans

---

[21] D. Scott Cormode, "A Financial History of Presbyterian Congregations Since World War II." In *The Organizational Revolution: Presbyterians and American Denominationalism* edited by Milton J Coalter, John M. Mulder, and Louis B. Weeks (Louisville, KY: Westminster/John Knox Press, 1992), 189.

[22] Kenneth W. Innskeep, "Giving Trends in the Evangelical Lutheran Church in America." In the *Review of Religious Research* 36, no. 2 (December 1994), 240-242.

[23] See for example, John A. Siewert and John A. Kenyon, eds., *Mission Handbook 1993-1995* (Monrovia, CA: MARC [Mission Advanced Research Center], 1993).

[24] See *The State of Church Giving through 1993*, pages 85-86, for a discussion of the possible effects of a supportive culture on church member behavior.

being accompanied by only a slight decline in membership. The correlation of membership with per member giving to denominational overseas ministries for the five denominations was .88.

It may also be noted that between 1987 and 1991, per member giving in constant 1987 dollars to missions declined in both the Assemblies of God and the Southern Baptist Convention. At the same time, the rate of membership growth in both denominations slowed measurably. Analysis of an expanded set of denominations would provide useful information about the strength of the observed relationship between missions support and membership patterns.

Figure 12: **A Comparison of the Percent Change in Per Member Giving in Constant 1987 $ to Denominational Overseas Ministries and Membership in Five Protestant Denominations, 1972 to 1991**

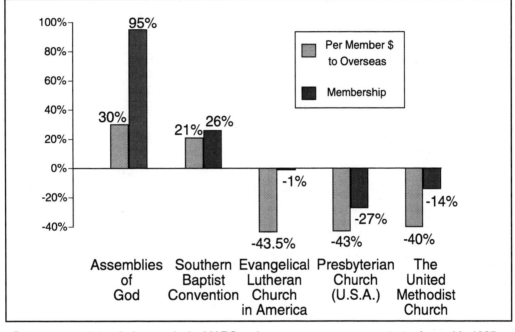

Sources: empty tomb, inc. analysis; MARC series;   empty tomb graphic 1995
        YACC adjusted series

"Denominational Reports and Other Estimates of Charitable Giving" (from *The State of Church Giving through 1993*[25])

In presentations, members of the audience not uncommonly express confusion about information regarding church member giving declines in light of other estimates of charitable giving. One source of widely-published data is the American Association of Fund-Raising Counsel, Inc. annual series, *Giving USA*. The other is the Independent Sector biannual series, *Giving and Volunteers in the United States*. Church member giving data can be used in an attempt to provide external validation with the findings of the AAFRC and Independent Sector publications.

---

[25] See also *The State of Church Giving through 1989* and *The State of Church Giving through 1991*.

In summary, the Independent Sector data is from a Gallup survey of individuals about their giving habits. The AAFRC data is a set of estimates prepared by an organization of professional fund-raising organizations. The *State of Church Giving* series published by empty tomb has considered the estimates of giving in comparison with church member giving data.[26] In the present discussion, only brief highlights will be reviewed.

One comparison can be made in giving to religion across time. Data from Independent Sector studies, AAFRC reports and for 28 denominations reporting in the *YACC* series is available for the years 1987, 1989, 1991 and 1993. By aggregating the average household contribution to religion in the Independent Sector results, a giving to religion figure can be obtained to compare with the AAFRC religion total and the total received by the 28 denominations reporting to the *YACC*. The trends provide a basis of comparison about what these three sources are saying regarding giving to religion.

The analysis found that the Independent Sector data suggests that total religious giving increased 30% from 1987 to 1989, decreased by 12% from 1989 to 1991, and then held steady between 1991 and 1993. The AAFRC data indicates giving to religion increased by 10% between 1987 and 1989, increased by 13% between 1989 and 1991, and then increased by 4% between 1991 and 1993. The denominational reports for the set of 28 denominations indicate an increase of 10% between 1987 and 1989, an increase of 8% between 1989 and 1991, and an increase of 6% between 1991 and 1993. See Table 16 for a presentation of this data.

Table 16: **Estimates of Religious Giving and Percent Change, Independent Sector, AAFRC, and 28 *YACC* Denominations, 1987, 1989, 1991 and 1993, in Current Dollars**

Year	Independent Sector		AAFRC		YACC Set of 28 Denominations	
	Giving to Religion (in billions)	Percent Change from Previous Base	Giving to Religion (in billions)	Percent Change from Previous Base	Giving to Religion (in billions)	Percent Change from Previous Base
1987	$34.2		$43.5		$14.6	
1989	$44.5	30%	$47.8	10%	$16.0	10%
1991	$39.2	-12%	$53.9	13%	$17.4	8%
1993	$39.0	0%	$56.3	4%	$18.5	6%

Details in the above table may not compute to the numbers shown due to rounding.

It may not be surprising that the AAFRC data follows a pattern similar to that of the *YACC* denominations, since AAFRC revised its 1987 through 1990 estimates of giving to religion by using in part the rate of change in a set of *YACC* denominations, and then applied linear regression to calculate 1991 and 1992 estimates based on the 1987 to 1990 pattern.[27] A similar approach has subsequently been used to develop estimates for more recent years.

---

[26] For a detailed discussion of how Independent Sector income data compares to the U.S. Bureau of the Census figures, and how Independent Sector giving to education compares to Council for Aid to Education estimates, see *The State of Church Giving through 1993*, 47-51.

[27] Ann E. Kaplan, ed., *Giving USA 1993* (New York: American Association of Fund-Raising Counsel Trust for Philanthropy, 1993), 188.

The denominational data can also be used to validate findings by specific denomination, as noted in the following excerpt from *The State of Church Giving through 1993.*

> ***Methodists Validation Trial.*** Table [17 below] presents data on giving by Methodists. As noted earlier, Independent Sector indicates that "the error rate could be much larger for small portions of the sample, particularly when only a small percentage of respondents report giving and volunteering to a certain area."[28] However, the data published in the *Giving and Volunteering* series may still be used and quoted by practitioners and others in spite of that caveat. Were Independent Sector's sample for specific large denominations such that the error rate were within acceptable limits, it would be possible to conduct validation trials of its survey instrument. Table [17] compares Independent Sector findings for Methodists with the largest Methodist denomination in the U.S., The United Methodist Church, which is the second largest Protestant communion, and which represented 3.35% of the U.S. population in 1993. This denomination is an example of one of the five or so large denominations which could each be used in a validation trial.

> The Independent Sector Methodist data in Table [17] was derived as follows. The Independent Sector estimate for the percentage of Methodist respondents was multiplied by the number of households in the United States for the appropriate year. The resulting number of Methodist households was multiplied by the current dollar household contribution by Methodists, to yield a Total Contributions by Methodist households figure. The U.S. population for the relevant year was multiplied by the percentage of Methodist respondents in the Independent Sector survey to yield a Methodist population figure. The aggregated Total Contributions by Methodist households figure was then divided by the Methodist population figure to produce a per capita Methodist figure.[29]

> A review of the data yielded the following patterns. The Independent Sector data suggested an increased contribution from 1987 to 1989, a decrease from 1989 to 1991, and a slight increase from 1991 to 1993. The United Methodist Church data posted an increase from 1987 to 1989, from 1989 to 1991, and again from 1991 to 1993.

> The Independent Sector data measured the equivalent of inclusive membership contributions to the church, as well as any contributions made by Methodists to other religious and nonreligious charitable organizations. The United Methodist data measured largely contributions of full or confirmed members specifically to the congregation. Such a distinction highlights the fact that, were the proposed Independent Sector validation trial question framed so that it asked respondents for the amount contributed to their local congregation in one question, and to other philanthropy categories in a separate question, a sharper comparison could be made between Independent Sector survey findings and published denominational data which summarizes congregational giving.

> In this trial, the Independent Sector findings that Methodist per capita constant dollar contributions increased 64% between 1987 and 1989, decreased 31% between 1989 and

---

[28] Virginia Hodgkinson and Murray S. Weitzman, eds., *Giving and Volunteering* (Washington, DC: Independent Sector, 1994), xii.

[29] The Independent Sector data is from the following editions of Hodgkinson and Weitzman, *Giving and Volunteering*: 1987 data, 1988 edition, page 17, (Methodist percent of population of 9.1% from correspondence dated 9/29/93 from Heather A. Gorski, Research Associate of Independent Sector); 1989 data, 1990 edition, page 60; 1991 data, 1992 edition, page 76; 1993 data, 1994 edition, Volume I, page 115. The United Methodist Church membership and financial data is from the relevant edition of the *Yearbook of American and Canadian Churches* (Nashville, TN: Abingdon Press).

1991, and increased 3% between 1991 and 1993, need to be reviewed in light of The United Methodist Church reports indicating that full or confirmed per member contributions increased 3% between 1987 and 1989, 0% between 1989 and 1991, and 2% between 1991 and 1993 (see Table 17).

Table 17: **Validation Trial Comparing Independent Sector Methodist Data with Data for The United Methodist Church**

| Year | Independent Sector Methodist Contributions to All Causes | | | | Contributions to The United Methodist Church Congregations | | | |
| | Total Current Dollars (billions) | Per Capita | | | Total Current Dollars (billions) | Per Full/Confirmed Member | | |
		Current Dollars	Constant '93 Dollars CPI 82-4=100	% Change in Constant $, from Previous Base		Current Dollars	Constant '93 Dollars CPI 82-4=100	% Change in Constant $, from Previous Base
1987	$3.8	$173	$220		$2.6	$284	$362	
1989	$7.4	$310	$361	64%	$2.8	$320	$372	3%
1991	$5.7	$235	$250	-31%	$3.1	$353	$374	0%
1993	$6.4	$258	$258	3%	$3.3	$382	$382	2%

Details in the above table may not compute to the numbers shown due to rounding.

The AFFRC giving to religion estimate for 1987 through the present is based on a projection which incorporates a rate of change in selected denominations from the *YACC* series. However, in previous years, the estimate for giving to religion was considered a residual category.[30] That is, whatever charitable contributions were not attributable to another category were attributed to religion. While AAFRC has changed its methodology in recent years, no adjustment to the years in which Religion was regarded as a residual category has been made. Thus the category of Religion, which is the single largest AAFRC charitable giving category, is cumulatively built on the data years in which religion was a residual category.

The following excerpt from *The State of Church Giving through 1993* considers an adjusted estimate for the AAFRC religion figures.

> ***Trends in the AAFRC Estimate of Giving to Religion.*** Lacking the type of information discussed above in "The Need for Data Sources for the AAFRC Estimates of Giving" section, it is difficult to analyze the accuracy of the AAFRC estimates of giving for the specific Use of Contribution category of Religion. Nevertheless, one possible approach is to develop an update formula from another source of accessible data and apply that update to past *Giving USA* data for Religion, to calculate a 1993 estimate. The calculated 1993 estimate thus arrived at can be compared to the published AAFRC estimate, to see how the calculated estimate compares with the results of the formula that AAFRC uses

---

[30] Nathan Weber, ed., *Giving USA 1990* (New York: American Association of Fund-Raising Counsel Trust for Philanthropy, 1990), 187.

Figure 13: **Estimates of Total Religious Giving in 1993, AAFRC, AAFRC Adjusted from 1974 by Denominational Rate of Change, and Independent Sector**

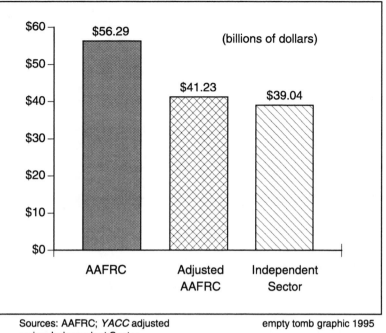

Sources: AAFRC; *YACC* adjusted series; Independent Sector

empty tomb graphic 1995

to produce its published Uses of Contributions category estimate.

As noted earlier, AAFRC pegged its 1960-1972 estimates of giving to the Filer Commission estimates for the Uses Categories of Education and Health. The 1974 AAFRC estimate for giving to Religion was $11.84 billion.[31] This figure was close to the Filer Commission estimate of $11.7 billion for giving to religion in 1974.[32] Therefore, adjusting the AAFRC estimate of the Religion Uses Category by another calculated estimate of change beginning in 1974 might provide a realistic estimate of giving to Religion in 1993, which can be compared with the current AAFRC projection for that year.

The composite group of 29 Protestant denominations for which data has been analyzed in other chapters of this report can serve as an external source for a percentage change in giving to religion. In fact, AAFRC methodology now states, "For the year 1987-1993, data on giving to a sample of large American congregations [sic] as documented in the *Yearbook of American and Canadian Churches* is used to calculate a percentage change from one year to the next."[33]Since the composite group of 29 Protestant denominations analyzed in the present report represents a broad cross section of denominations, it is reasonable to apply this same percentage of change to the 1974 estimate of giving to Religion, to obtain a comparable increase in the AAFRC estimate. These 29 denominations grew from $3.9 billion in 1974 to $13.6 billion in 1993 in current dollars. Thus, their income increased 248% from 1974 to 1993.

---

[31] Kaplan, 1993, 22.

[32] *Research Papers Sponsored by The Commission on Private Philanthropy and Public Needs, Vol. 1, History, Trends, and Current Magnitudes* (Washington, DC: Department of the Treasury, 1977), 136.

[33] Ann E. Kaplan, *Giving USA 1995* (New York: American Association of Fund-Raising Counsel Trust for Philanthropy, 1995), 175.

The rate of change reported by 29 denominations, when applied to the published AAFRC 1974 estimate of giving to Religion of $11.84 billion resulted in a figure of $41.23 billion for 1993.

The actual AAFRC estimate of giving to Religion in 1993 was $56.29 billion. This figure is a 375% increase from the 1974 AAFRC figure, compared to the 248% increase among the religious denominations. As a result, the AAFRC estimate of giving to Religion presented in *Giving USA 1995* is 37% greater than the estimate which resulted using the rate of change from 1974 to 1993 among 29 denominations based on their reported income.

Interestingly, the $41.2 billion estimate that resulted when the rate of change among the 29 denominations was applied to the AAFRC figure was 6% greater than the Independent Sector aggregate estimate of giving to Religion in 1993 of $39.04 billion. Figure [13] presents estimates of giving to religion in 1993 for AAFRC, the AAFRC data when adjusted from 1974 by the denominational rate of change, and for Independent Sector.

"Church Member Giving in Perspective: Can Church Members Afford to Give More?" (from *The State of Church Giving through 1992*)

The question is often raised as to whether church members can afford to give more, given the increased costs in such personal expenditure categories as health insurance and utilities. The changes in church member giving were compared to changes in other aspects of lifestyle expenditures to shed light on whether charitable giving is an economic possibility for many church members.

Data regarding details of new house starts suggested that expectations regarding housing square footage and other amenities increased between 1970 and 1992. Also, while church member giving as a percentage of income decreased between 1975 and 1991, and U.S. per capita income increased by 48%, credit card interest payments (not including purchases or fees) increased from $4.3 billion to $28.3 billion in constant 1987 dollars. On a per capita basis, these credit card interest payments increased from $21.42 to $112.00 per American, an increase of 423%.

A listing of average American consumer expenditures for selected items such as soft drinks, candy, video rentals and pet care totaled $1,602 in constant 1987 dollars. In contrast, 1992 per member giving to churches in constant 1987 dollars was $366 (see Table 18). While the comparison of per capita consumer expenditures is only approximate since the original source data years for consumer expenditures vary, the information nevertheless suggests that the discussion about whether church members can afford to give more to their churches needs to take into account the priorities set by church members as well as the issue of whether their incomes provide the economic resources to increase giving.

Table 18: Combined Per Capita Purchase of Selected Items Compared to Composite Per Member Church Giving, in Constant 1987 Dollars

Item Purchased (Source Year)	Per Capita Expenditure, Constant 1987 Dollars
Soft Drinks (1989)	$164
Candy (1988)	47
Ice Cream (1992)	32
Pizza (1992)	52
Purchased Meals/Beverages (1992)	657
Cosmetics (1992)	64
Sporting Goods (1992)	103
Cable TV (basic) (1992)	40
Movies (1992)	16
Video Rentals (1990)	37
Toys (1992)	45
Pet Food/Supplies (1992)	40
Pet Care/Veterinarian (1990)	21
Leisure Travel (1992)	129
Craft Sales (1992)	13
Coin-Operated Amusements (1991)	24
Home Video Games (1992)	20
Fishing (1990)	99
Total Leisure Spending	$1,602
1992 Per Member Church Giving	$366

Details in the above table may not compute to the numbers shown due to rounding.

"Church Member Giving in Recession Years: 1970, 1974, 1980, 1982 and 1990" (from *The State of Church Giving through 1990*)

An often-cited assumption is that "people can't afford to give" in difficult economic times.

A comparison was done of church member giving in first-year recession years in the 1968-1990 period to explore this assumption. There were five first-year recession years during this 23-year period: 1970, 1974, 1980, 1982 and 1990. The data shows that per member giving in constant 1982 dollars increased in three of the five first-year recession years to both Total Contributions and Congregational Finances. Per member giving in constant dollars increased to Benevolences in two of the five first-year recession years (see Table 19). This comparison would suggest that it may not be assumed that church members necessarily decrease giving in difficult economic times.

Table 19: **Church Member Giving in Constant 1982 Dollars, Comparing First-Year Recession Years with the Years Immediately Preceding, 1968-1990**

Year	Total Contributions		Congregational Finances		Benevolences	
(Recession Year in bold)	Per Member Dollar Contribution	Actual change in $	Per Member Dollar Contribution	Actual change in $	Per Member Dollar Contribution	Actual change in $
1969	251.25		197.27		53.98	
1970	**245.65**	(5.60)	**195.35**	(1.92)	**50.31**	(3.68)
1973	248.34		199.58		48.77	
1974	**252.54**	4.19	**201.89**	2.32	**50.64**	1.88
1979	260.48		209.25		51.23	
1980	**263.40**	2.92	**211.39**	2.15	**52.01**	0.77
1981	265.91		213.24		52.67	
1982	**269.22**	3.31	**218.60**	5.36	**50.62**	(2.05)
1989	305.92		251.44		54.47	
1990	**305.51**	(0.40)	**252.38**	0.94	**53.13**	(1.34)

Per Member Giving in Recession Years, in Constant 1982 Dollars spans across the three main contribution columns.

Details in the above table may not compute to the numbers shown due to rounding.

"Church Member Giving and U.S. Social Health"
(updated from *The State of Church Giving through 1990*[34])

As a major social institution, one might assume that the church is not only influenced by society, but also has an impact on the culture around it. One might further assume that the changes in church member giving could have an effect on the texture of society. Of course, although correlation does not necessarily indicate a causal relationship, correlations may suggest interesting relationships deserving of further analysis.

For example, per member giving to Benevolences may be termed the amount that church members are investing in the broader mission of the church, beyond the congregation's own operating expenses. As noted earlier, the level of per member giving in constant 1987 dollars to Benevolences was lower in the 1990s than in 1968. As a consequence, the portion of income directed to the category of Benevolences had also declined from the late 1960s to the early 1990s. How does this trend compare to a measure of U.S. social health?

Marc Miringoff, Director of the Fordham University Institute for Innovation in Social Policy, has produced a U.S. Social Health Index. This index measures 16 national statistics, including such factors as various forms of poverty; the rate of homicides; teenage suicide; and highway deaths due to alcohol. Beginning in 1970, the combined index of U.S. social health

---

[34] For a discussion of an earlier version of this comparison, see *The State of Church Giving through 1990* which considers data for 1970 to 1989..

measured 73.8. By 1992, the index had declined to 40.6, a decrease of 45% in the index measuring U.S. social health.[35]

Giving to Benevolences during the 1970 to 1992 period was compared. During the 1970 to 1992 period, per member giving as a percentage of income to Benevolences for the composite group of 29 denominations decreased from 0.60% to 0.44%, a decrease of 27%. Further analysis would be required to determine the strength of the correlation between the decline in social health and the decline in church member giving to Benevolences. However, the initial juxtaposition of the data suggests an intriguing avenue for exploration.

General Discussion of Approaches to Research.

In working with church data, a number of research-related, theoretical or philosophy of science issues have come to the fore in discussion from time to time.

Advocacy. Some in the world of religious studies, it seems, would question the relationship between advocacy and research. This seems somewhat curious, since for a number of decades, the position has been recognized in other fields that, given the fact that the observer normatively brings bias to research, perhaps the best one can do is to recognize one's bias, and, through the tools of research design and critical awareness, strive to guard against any systematic influence of one's bias.

Most research conducted by humans relates to values, however many steps removed a certain research project may be from a value-laden concern—whether it be in the realm of, for example, health, education or environment. As the late Abraham Maslow eloquently put it, "The classical philosophy of science as morally neutral, value free, value neutral is not only wrong, but is extremely dangerous..."[36] Even if one argues that a given hypothesis about, say black holes in outer space, is in fact value-free, the researcher may soon become personally invested in developing a given hypothesis or theory.

Applied vs. Basic Research. Turning to applied versus basic research—in many settings, basic research is contrasted with applied or industrial research.

It may be worth noting that, although the topics under consideration in the current presentation have to do with the "application" of denominational data, they nevertheless constitute "basic" research within the parameters of the field of religious studies. That is to say, to know whether giving goes up or down in a recession, how giving rates compare for evangelicals and mainline denominations, and the extent to which church giving data provides insights into other measures of philanthropy—to know the answers to these questions does not provide experimentally verified findings which can be applied, for example, by congregations or denominations in order to reverse declining giving and membership trends.

Correlational vs. Experimental Research. Finally, there are two core types of research. One has to do with correlational/sociological/ demographic analysis. The second

---

[35] Miringoff, Marc L., *1994, The Index of Social Health, Measuring the Social Well-Being of the Nation* (Tarrytown, NY: Fordham University Institute for Innovation in Social Policy, 1994), 4

[36] Karl Menninger, M.D., *Whatever Became of Sin?* (New York: Hawthorne Books, 1973), 215.

has to do with the introduction of variable conditions and evaluation of the results.

Correlational research is an often weaker form of research than the introduction of experimental conditions in controlled settings. This is so because it is more difficult to determine cause and effect in correlational studies. Sociological studies employ correlational, factor analysis and multiple regression research techniques, in part, because the large society-wide variables it examines are difficult to reduce to experimental settings—although, among the social sciences, social psychology bridges the gap to some extent between sociology with its correlational analyses and psychology with its experience with experimental design.

Religious research studies have tended to emphasize the correlational/ demographic approach in comparison to the experimental approach.

The religious research studies' focus on correlational vs. experimental analysis is understandable insofar as research has been focused on church membership. First, membership goes to the heart of doctrinal, theological distinctions between denominations. Second, in a highly churched society, membership is necessarily, and by definition, competitive—with comparatively little room for major growth. Third-party experimental analysis in any way favoring one group over another could be a volatile, highly controversial undertaking when discussing membership categories.

A focus on church giving, in contrast to membership—even though there may be a relationship between giving and membership—lends itself to experimental research more easily because it is not inherently a competitive situation among congregations or denominations at a primary level. Increased giving within a congregation does not decrease giving within another congregation, whereas increasing membership in one congregation can impact membership in another congregation. Concerns about church giving are primarily addressed within an already-constituted membership. In addition, carrying out giving experiments interdenominationally assures each body that one group is not excluded from gaining information in a timely fashion that would be possibly useful to another.

Applying the findings of correlational research has rightly been seen as a responsibility of the end-users—in the case of religious research, that being congregations and denominations. For example, if a correlational study finds that 10% of the variation in church attendance is accounted for by whether or not churches have signs by a main road, then it is up to a congregation or denomination to apply these results or not.

However, this correct assumption that a congregation needs to apply the findings of correlational studies can be confused with the role for experimental research which tests theories. In this example, a correlational study suggests that congregations with signs have higher levels of attendance. An experimental research project would locate 60 congregations without signs in comparable locations and arrange for 30 to install signs. Monitoring attendance over the next year would help determine if the hypothesis suggested by the correlation—that congregations without signs can improve attendance by installing signs— is true, or if some other factor was operating in the initial set of congregations in the correlation study.

ORDER FORM

Reprints of special focus chapters from previous editions of *The State of Church Giving* series are available. If you would like a copy of the complete text of one of the chapters summarized on the previous pages, please fill out the form below and return it to the empty tomb office. All prices include postage and handling.

This form may be photocopied for purposes of ordering the listed documents.

Please send me the documents indicated below. Enclosed is my payment.

Your name:_____ Institution:_____

Mailing Address: _____

| | | Street or P.O. Box | City | State | Zip |

	Chapter	Price per Copy	# Ordered	Total Cost
❏	"An Exploration of Roman Catholic Giving Patterns" (from *The State Church Giving through 1993*)	$5.00	_____	_____
❏	"A Unified Theory of Church Giving and Membership" (from *The State of Church Giving through 1993*)	$5.00	_____	_____
❏	"Denominational Reports and Other Estimates of Charitable Giving" (a set of three papers from *The State of Church through 1989*, *The State of Church Giving through 1991* and *The State of Church Giving through 1993*)	$12.00	_____	_____
❏	"Church Giving in Perspective: Can Church Members Afford to Give More?" (from *The State of Church Giving through 1992*)	$5.00	_____	_____
❏	"Church Member Giving in Recession Years: 1970, 1974, 1980, 1982 and 1990" (from *The State of Church Giving through 1990*)	$5.00	_____	_____
❏	"Church Member Giving and U.S. Social Health" (from *The State of Church Giving through 1990*; considers data for 1970-1989)	$5.00	_____	_____
	TOTAL			_____

Please return a copy of this form and a check made out to empty tomb, inc. in the amount on the TOTAL line to: empty tomb, inc.
P.O. Box 2404
Champaign, IL 61825-2404

Appendix A: List of Denominations

Church Member Giving, 1968-1994

American Baptist Churches in the U.S.A.
Associate Reformed Presbyterian Church
  (General Synod)
Brethren in Christ Church
Christian Church (Disciples of Christ)
Church of God (Anderson, Ind.)
Church of God General Conference (Oregon, Ill.)
Church of the Brethren
Church of the Nazarene
Conservative Congregational Christian Conference
Cumberland Presbyterian Church
Evangelical Congregational Church
Evangelical Covenant Church
Evangelical Lutheran Church in America
  The American Lutheran Church (merged 1987)
  Lutheran Church in America (merged 1987)
Evangelical Lutheran Synod
Evangelical Mennonite Church
Fellowship of Evangelical Bible Churches
Free Methodist Church of North America
Friends United Meeting (through 1990)
General Association of General Baptists
Lutheran Church-Missouri Synod
Mennonite Church
Moravian Church in America, Northern Province
North American Baptist Conference
The Orthodox Presbyterian Church
Presbyterian Church (U.S.A.)
Reformed Church in America
Seventh-day Adventists
Southern Baptist Convention
United Church of Christ
Wisconsin Evangelical Lutheran Synod

Church Member Giving, 1993–1994

The Denominations included in the 1968-1994
  analysis plus the following:
Allegheny Wesleyan Methodist Connection
  (Original Allegheny Conference)
Baptist Missionary Alliance
Christian Missionary and Alliance
Church of the Lutheran Confession
Churches of God General Conference
The Episcopal Church
The Evangelical Church
Evangelical Presbyterian Church
General Association of Regular Baptist Churches
International Pentecostal Church of Christ
The Latvian Evangelical Lutheran Church in America

Mennonite Church, The General Conference
Missionary Church, Inc.
Primitive Methodist Church in the U.S.A.
The Schwenkfelder Church
United Brethren in Christ
The United Methodist Church
The Wesleyan Church

By Organizational Affiliation: NAE, 1968-1994

Brethren in Christ Church
Church of the Nazarene
Conservative Congregational Christian Conference
Evangelical Congregational Church
Evangelical Mennonite Church
Fellowship of Evangelical Bible Churches
Free Methodist Church of North America
General Association of General Baptists

By Organizational Affiliation: NCC, 1968-1994

American Baptist Churches in the U.S.A.
Christian Church (Disciples of Christ)
Church of the Brethren
Evangelical Lutheran Church in America
Moravian Church in America, Northern Province
Presbyterian Church (U.S.A.)
Reformed Church in America
United Church of Christ

Eleven Denominations, 1921-1994

American Baptist (Northern)
Christian Church (Disciples of Christ)
Church of the Brethren
The Episcopal Church
Evangelical Lutheran Church in America
  The American Lutheran Church
    American Lutheran Church
    The Evangelical Lutheran Church
    United Evangelical Lutheran Church
    Lutheran Free Church
  Evangelical Lutheran Churches, Assn. of
  Lutheran Church in America
    United Lutheran Church
      General Council Evangelical Lutheran Ch.
      General Synod of Evangelical Lutheran Ch.
      United Synod Evangelical Lutheran South
    American Evangelical Lutheran Church
    Augustana Lutheran Church
    Finnish Lutheran Church (Suomi Synod)

Moravian Church in America, Northern Province
Presbyterian Church (U.S.A.)
   United Presbyterian Church in the U.S.A.
     Presbyterian Church in the U.S.A.
     United Presbyterian Church in North America
   Presbyterian Church in the U.S.
Reformed Church in America
Southern Baptist Convention
United Church of Christ
   Congregational Christian
     Congregational
   Evangelical and Reformed
     Evangelical Synod of North America/German
     Reformed Church in the U.S.
The United Methodist Church
   The Evangelical United Brethren
   The Methodist Church
     Methodist Episcopal Church
     Methodist Episcopal Church South
     Methodist Protestant Church

Fellowship of Evan. Bible Churches
Free Methodist Church of North America
General Association of General Baptists
Lutheran Church-Missouri Synod
Mennonite Church
North American Baptist Conference
The Orthodox Presbyterian Church
Salvation Army
Seventh-day Adventists
Southern Baptist Convention
Wisconsin Evangelical Lutheran Synod

Trends in Membership, 10 Mainline Protestant Denominations, 1968-1994

American Baptist Churches in the U.S.A.
Christian Church (Disciples of Christ)
Church of the Brethren
The Episcopal Church
Evangelical Lutheran Church in Am.
Moravian Church in America, Northern Prov.
Presbyterian Church (U.S.A.)
Reformed Church in America
United Church of Christ
The United Methodist Church

Trends in Membership, Add 26 Denominations, 1968-1994

Assemblies of God
Associate Reformed Presby. Ch (Gen Synod)
Baptist General Conference
Brethren in Christ Church
Christian and Missionary Alliance
Church of God (Anderson, IN)
Church of God (Cleveland, Tenn.)
Church of God, Gen. Conf. (Oregon, IL)
Church of the Nazarene
Conservative Cong. Christian Conf.
Cumberland Presbyterian Church
Evangelical Congregational Church
Evangelical Covenant Church
Evangelical Lutheran Synod
Evangelical Mennonite Church

Appendix B Series: Denominational Data Tables

Introduction

The data in the following tables is from the *Yearbook of American and Canadian Churches* (*YACC*) series unless otherwise noted. Financial data is presented in current dollars.

The Appendix B tables are described below.

Appendix B-1, Church Member Giving, 1968-1994: This table presents data for the denominations which comprise the data set analyzed for the 1968 through 1994 period.

Elements of this data are also used for the analyses in the Church Member Giving for Eleven Denominations, 1921-1994 section; the Church Member Giving, 1993-1994 section; and the Church Member Giving in Denominations Defined by Organizational Affiliation section.

In Appendix B-1, the data for the Presbyterian Church (U.S.A.) combined data for the United Presbyterian Church in the U.S.A. and the Presbyterian Church in the United States for the period 1968 through 1982. These two communions merged to become the Presbyterian Church (U.S.A.) in 1983, data for which is presented for 1983 through 1994.

Also in Appendix B-1, data for the Evangelical Lutheran Church in America appears beginning in 1987. Before that, the two major component communions that merged into that new denomination—the American Lutheran Church and the Lutheran Church in America—are listed as individual denominations from 1968 through 1986.

In the Appendix B series, the denomination listed as the Fellowship of Evangelical Bible Churches had been named the Evangelical Mennonite Brethren Church prior to July 1987.

Revised data for one or more years became available for one denominations, resulting in minor changes in the data set. In addition, as of the previous edition in this series, more extensive revisions were made in the data of two denominations as follows.

Data for the American Baptist Churches in the U.S.A. has been obtained directly from the denominational office as follows. In discussions with the American Baptist Churches Office of Planning Resources, it became apparent that there had been no distinction made between the membership of congregations reporting financial data, and total membership for the denomination, when reporting data to the *Yearbook of American and Canadian Churches*. Records were obtained from the denomination for a smaller membership figure that reflected only those congregations reporting financial data. While this revised membership data provided a more useful per member giving figure for Congregational Finances, the total Benevolences figure reported to the *YACC*, while included in the present data set, does reflect contributions to some Benevolences categories from 100% of the American Baptist membership. The membership reported in Appendix B-1 for the American Baptist Churches is the membership for congregations reporting financial data, rather than the total membership figure provided in editions of the *Yearbook of American and Canadian Churches*. However, in the sections that consider membership as a percentage of population, the Total Membership figure for the American Baptist Churches is used.

The Reformed Church in America data reported in the *YACC* was compared to denominational journals for the period 1968 through 1994. In communication with the denominational office, a staff person stated that records submitted to the *YACC* as U.S. data included data for some Canadian congregations that are members of the Reformed Church in America. Since the present study focuses on congregations in the U.S., copies of denominational journals were obtained, and, as necessary, records for Canadian congregations in the Reformed Church in America were subtracted to obtain U.S. only data.

Appendix B-2, Church Member Giving, 1993-1994: Appendix B-2 presents the Full or Confirmed Membership, Congregational Finances and Benevolences data for the eighteen additional denominations included in the 1993-1994 comparison.

Appendix B-3, Church Member Giving for Eleven Denominations, 1921-1994: This appendix presents additional data which is not included in Appendix B-1 for the Eleven Denominations.

The data from 1921 through 1928 in Appendix B-3.1 is taken from summary information contained in the *Yearbook of American Churches, 1949 Edition*, George F. Ketcham, ed. (Lebanon, PA: Sowers Printing Company, 1949, p. 162). The summary membership data provided is for Inclusive Membership. Therefore, giving as a percentage of income for the years 1921 through 1928 may have been somewhat higher had Full or Confirmed Membership been used. The list of denominations that are summarized for this period is presented in the *Yearbook of American Churches, 1953 Edition*, Benson Y. Landis, ed. (New York: National Council of the Churches of Christ in the U.S.A., 1953, p. 274).

The data from 1929 through 1952 is taken from summary information presented in the *Yearbook of American Churches, Edition for 1955*, Benson Y. Landis, ed. (New York: National Council of the Churches of Christ in the U.S.A., 1954, pp. 286-287). A description of the list of denominations included in the 1929 through 1952 data summary on page 275 of the *YACC Edition for 1955* indicated that the Moravian Church, Northern Province is not included in the 1929 through 1952 data.

The data in Appendix B-3.2 for 1953 through 1964 was obtained for the indicated denominations from the relevant edition of the *YACC* series. Giving as a percentage of income was derived for these years by dividing the published Total Contributions figure by the published Per Capita figure to produce a membership figure for each denomination. The Total Contributions figures for the denominations were added to produce an aggregated Total Contributions figure. The calculated membership figures were also added to produce an aggregated membership figure. The aggregated Total Contributions figure was then divided by the aggregated membership figure to yield a per member giving figure which was used in calculating giving as a percentage of income.

Data for the years 1965 through 1967 was not available in a form that could be readily analyzed for the present purposes, and therefore data for these three years was estimated by dividing the change in per capita Total Contributions from 1964 to 1968 by four, the number of years in this interval, and cumulatively adding the result to the base year of 1964 and the succeeding years of 1965 and 1966 to obtain estimates for the years 1965 through 1967.

In most cases, this procedure was also applied to individual denominations to avoid an artificially low total due to missing data. If data was not available for a specific year, the otherwise blank entry was filled in with a calculation based on surrounding years for that denomination. For example, this procedure was used for the American Baptist Churches for the years 1955 and 1956, the Christian Church (Disciples of Christ) for the years 1955 and 1959, and the Evangelical United Brethren, later to merge into The United Methodist Church, for the years 1957, 1958 and 1959. Data for the Methodist Church was changed for 1957 in a similar manner.

Available Total Contributions and Full or Confirmed Members data for The Episcopal Church and The United Methodist Church for 1969 through 1994 is presented in Appendix B-3.3. These two communions are included in the Eleven Denominations. The United Methodist Church was created in 1968 when The Methodist Church and The Evangelical United Brethren Church merged. While The Methodist Church filed summary data for the year 1968, The Evangelical United Brethren Church did not. Data for these denominations was calculated as noted in the appendix. However, since the 1968 data for The Methodist Church would not have been comparable to the 1985 and 1994 data for The United Methodist Church, this communion was not included in the more focused 1968-1994 analysis.

Appendix B-4, Trends in Giving and Membership: Appendix B-4.1 lists membership data for denominations included in these analyses which is not included in another appendix.

Appendix B-1: Church Member Giving 1968-1994

Key to Denominational Abbreviations: Data Years 1968-1994

Abbreviation	Denomination
abc	American Baptist Churches in the U.S.A.
alc	The American Lutheran Church
arp	Associate Reformed Presbyterian Church (General Synod)
bcc	Brethren in Christ Church
ccd	Christian Church (Disciples of Christ)
cga	Church of God (Anderson, IN)
cgg	Church of God General Conference (Oregon, IL)
chb	Church of the Brethren
chn	Church of the Nazarene
ccc	Conservative Congregational Christian Conference
cpc	Cumberland Presbyterian Church
ecc	Evangelical Congregational Church
ecv	Evangelical Covenant Church
elc	Evangelical Lutheran Church in America
els	Evangelical Lutheran Synod
emc	Evangelical Mennonite Church
feb	Fellowship of Evangelical Bible Churches
fmc	Free Methodist Church of North America
fum	Friends United Meeting
ggb	General Association of General Baptists
lca	Lutheran Church in America
lms	Lutheran Church-Missouri Synod
mch	Mennonite Church
mca	Moravian Church in America, Northern Province
nab	North American Baptist Conference
opc	The Orthodox Presbyterian Church
pch	Presbyterian Church (U.S.A.)
rca	Reformed Church in America
sda	Seventh-day Adventists
sbc	Southern Baptist Convention
ucc	United Church of Christ
wel	Wisconsin Evangelical Lutheran Synod

Appendix B-1: Church Member Giving, 1968-1994 (continued)

	Data Year 1968			Data Year 1969			Data Year 1970		
	Full/Confirmed Members	Congregational Finances	Benevolences	Full/Confirmed Members	Congregational Finances	Benevolences	Full/Confirmed Members	Congregational Finances	Benevolences
abc	1,179,848 a	95,878,267 a	21,674,924 a	1,153,785 a	104,084,322	21,111,333	1,231,944 a	112,668,310	19,655,391
alc	1,767,618	137,260,390	32,862,410	1,771,999	143,917,440	34,394,570	1,775,573	146,268,320	30,750,030
arp	28,312	2,239,825	1,274,348	28,273	2,943,214	978,097	NA	NA	NA
bcc	8,954	1,645,256	633,200 a	9,145	1,795,859	817,445	NA	NA	NA
ccd	994,683	105,803,222	21,703,947	936,931	91,169,842	18,946,815	911,964	98,671,692	17,386,032
oga	146,807	23,310,682	4,168,580	147,752	24,828,448	4,531,678	150,198	26,962,037	4,886,223
cgg	6,600	805,000	103,000	6,700	805,000	104,000	6,800	810,000	107,000
chb	187,957	12,975,829	4,889,727	185,198	13,964,158 a	4,921,991 a	182,614	14,327,896	4,891,618
chn	364,789	59,943,750 a	14,163,761 a	372,943	64,487,669 a	15,220,339 a	383,284	68,877,922 a	16,221,123 a
ccc	15,127	1,867,978	753,686	16,219	1,382,195	801,534	17,328	1,736,818	779,696
cpc	86,729 a	5,542,678 a	906,583 a	88,091	6,393,665	1,020,248	NA	NA	NA
ecc	29,239	2,464,760	610,056	29,582	2,660,674	627,732	NA	NA	NA
ecv	66,021	11,923,084	3,072,848	67,522	12,168,837	3,312,306	67,441	13,309,618	3,578,876
elc	ALC & LCA	ALC & LCA	ALC & LCA	ALC & LCA	ALC & LCA	ALC & LCA	ALC & LCA	ALC & LCA	ALC & LCA
els	10,886 a	844,235 a	241,949 a	11,079	1,003,746	315,325	11,030	969,625	295,349
emc	2,870 a	447,397	232,331	NA	NA	NA	NA	NA	NA
feb	1,712 a	156,789 a	129,818 a	3,324	389,000	328,000	3,698	381,877	706,398
fmc	47,831 a	12,032,016 a	2,269,677 a	47,954 a	9,152,729	7,495,653	64,901	9,641,202	7,985,264
fum	55,469 a	3,564,793	1,256,192	55,257	3,509,509	1,289,026	53,970	3,973,802	1,167,183
ggb	65,000	4,303,183 a	269,921 a	NA	NA	NA	NA	NA	NA
lca	2,279,383	166,337,149	39,981,858	2,193,321	161,958,669	46,902,225	2,187,015	169,795,380	42,118,870
lms	1,877,799	178,042,762	47,415,800	1,900,708	185,827,626	49,402,590	1,922,569	193,352,322	47,810,664
mch	85,682	7,304,585 a	5,179,023 a	85,343	7,398,182	6,038,730	NA	NA	NA
mca	27,772	2,583,354	444,610	27,617	2,642,529	456,182	27,173	2,704,105	463,219
nab	42,371 a	5,176,669 a	1,383,964 a	55,100	6,681,410	2,111,588	55,080	6,586,929	2,368,288
opc	9,197	1,638,437	418,102	9,276	1,761,242	464,660	NA	NA	NA
pch	4,180,093	375,248,474	102,622,450	4,118,664	388,268,169	97,897,522	4,041,813	401,785,731	93,927,852
rca	226,819 a	25,410,489 a	9,197,642 a	224,992 a	27,139,579 a	9,173,312 a	223,353 a	29,421,849 a	9,479,503 a
sda	395,159 a	36,976,280	95,178,335	407,766	40,378,426	102,730,594	420,419	45,280,059	109,569,241
sbc	11,332,229 a	666,924,020 a	128,023,731 a	11,487,708	709,246,590	133,203,885	11,628,032	753,510,973	138,480,329
ucc	2,032,648 a	152,301,536	18,869,136	1,997,898	152,791,512	27,338,543	1,960,608	155,248,767	26,934,289
wel	259,954 a	19,000,023	6,574,308 a	265,069	20,786,613	6,417,042	271,117	22,582,545	6,810,612
Total	27,815,558	2,119,952,912	566,506,217	27,705,216	2,189,536,854	598,352,965	27,597,924	2,278,867,779	586,373,050

[a] Data obtained from denominational source.

72

Appendix B-1: Church Member Giving, 1968-1994 (continued)

	Data Year 1971			Data Year 1972			Data Year 1973		
	Full/Confirmed Members	Congregational Finances	Benevolences	Full/Confirmed Members	Congregational Finances	Benevolences	Full/Confirmed Members	Congregational Finances	Benevolences
abc	1,223,735 [a]	114,673,805	18,878,769	1,176,092 [a]	118,446,573	18,993,440	1,190,455 [a]	139,357,611	20,537,388
alc	1,775,774	146,324,460	28,321,740	1,773,414	154,786,570	30,133,850	1,770,119	168,194,730	35,211,440
arp	NA	NA	NA	NA	NA	NA	NA	NA	NA
bcc	9,550	2,357,786	851,725	9,730	2,440,400	978,957	NA	NA	NA
ccd	884,929	94,091,862	17,770,799	881,467	105,763,511	18,323,685	868,895	112,526,538	19,800,843
cga	152,787	28,343,604	5,062,282	155,920	31,580,751	5,550,487	157,828	34,649,592	6,349,695
cgg	7,200	860,000	120,000	7,400	900,000	120,000	7,440	940,000	120,000
chb	181,183	14,535,274	5,184,768	179,641	14,622,319 [b]	5,337,277 [b]	179,333	16,474,758	6,868,927
chn	394,197	75,107,918 [a]	17,859,332 [a]	404,732	82,891,903 [a]	20,119,679 [a]	417,200	91,318,469 [a]	22,661,140 [a]
ccc	19,416	1,903,865	937,572	20,400	1,983,364	1,002,765	21,014	2,116,291	1,066,277
cpc	57,147	6,848,115	1,139,480	56,212	8,449,593	554,843	56,584	9,715,351	847,727
ecc	29,652	3,001,867	646,187	29,682	3,563,512	742,292	29,434	3,469,890	798,968
ecv	68,428	14,857,190	3,841,887	69,815	14,557,206	4,169,053	69,922	15,500,129	4,259,950
elc	ALC & LCA	ALC & LCA	ALC & LCA	ALC & LCA	ALC & LCA	ALC & LCA	ALC & LCA	ALC & LCA	ALC & LCA
els	11,427	1,028,629	314,843	11,532	1,138,953	275,941	12,525	1,296,326	361,882
emc	NA	NA	NA	NA	NA	NA	3,131	593,070	408,440
feb	NA	NA	NA	NA	NA	NA	NA	NA	NA
fmc	65,040	13,863,601	6,092,503	48,455	15,206,381	6,638,789	48,763 [a]	17,483,258	7,000,353
fum	54,522	3,888,064	1,208,062	54,927	4,515,463	1,297,088	57,690	5,037,848	1,327,439
ggb	NA	NA	NA	NA	NA	NA	NA	NA	NA
lca	2,175,378	179,570,467	43,599,913	2,165,591	188,387,949	45,587,481	2,169,341	200,278,486	34,627,978
lms	1,945,889	203,619,804	48,891,368	1,963,262	216,756,345	50,777,670	1,983,114	230,435,598	54,438,074
mch	88,522	8,171,316	7,035,750	89,505	9,913,176	7,168,664	90,967	9,072,858	6,159,740
mca	26,101	2,576,172	459,447	25,500	2,909,252	465,316	25,468	3,020,667	512,424
nab	54,997	7,114,457	2,293,692	54,441	7,519,558	2,253,158	41,516	6,030,352	1,712,092
opc	NA	NA	NA	NA	NA	NA	NA	NA	NA
pch	3,963,665	420,865,807	93,164,548	3,855,494	436,042,890	92,691,469	3,730,312 [c]	480,735,088 [c]	95,462,247 [c]
rca	219,915 [a]	32,217,319 [a]	9,449,655 [a]	217,583 [a]	34,569,874 [a]	9,508,818 [a]	212,906 [a]	39,524,443 [a]	10,388,619 [a]
sda	433,906	49,208,043	119,913,879	449,188	54,988,781	132,411,980	464,276	60,643,602	149,994,942
sbc	11,824,676	814,406,626	160,510,775	12,065,333	896,427,208	174,711,648	12,295,400	1,011,467,569	193,511,983
ucc	1,928,674	158,924,956	26,409,521	1,895,016	165,556,364	27,793,561	1,867,810	168,602,602	28,471,058
wel	275,500	24,365,692	7,481,644	278,442	26,649,585	8,232,320	283,130	29,450,094	8,650,699
Total	27,872,210	2,422,726,699	627,440,141	27,938,774	2,600,567,481	665,840,231	28,054,573	2,857,935,220	711,550,325

[a] Data obtained from denominational source.

[b] YACC Church of the Brethren figures reported for 15 months due to fiscal year change; adjusted here to 12/15ths.

[c] The Presbyterian Church (USA) data for 1973 combines United Presbyterian Church in the U.S.A. data for 1973 (see YACC 1975) and an average of Presbyterian Church in the United States data for 1972 and 1974, since 1973 data was not reported in the YACC series.

Appendix B-1: Church Member Giving, 1968-1994 (continued)

	Data Year 1974			Data Year 1975			Data Year 1976		
	Full/Confirmed Members	Congregational Finances	Benevolences	Full/Confirmed Members	Congregational Finances	Benevolences	Full/Confirmed Members	Congregational Finances	Benevolences
abc	1,176,989 a	147,022,280	21,847,285	1,180,793 a	153,697,091	23,638,372	1,142,773 a	163,134,092	25,792,357
alc	1,764,186	173,318,574	38,921,546	1,764,810	198,863,519	75,666,809	1,768,758	215,527,544	76,478,278
arp	28,570	3,753,120	1,050,697	28,589	4,090,321	961,760	28,581	4,370,831	1,118,783
bcc	10,255	3,002,218	1,078,576	10,784	3,495,152	955,845	11,375	4,088,492	1,038,484
ccd	854,844	119,434,435	20,818,434	859,885	126,553,931	22,126,459	845,058	135,008,269	23,812,274
cga	161,401	39,189,287	7,343,123	166,259	42,077,029	7,880,559	170,285	47,191,302	8,854,295
cgg	7,455	975,000	105,000	7,485	990,000	105,000	7,620	1,100,000	105,000
chb	179,387	18,609,614	7,281,551	179,336	20,338,351	7,842,819 b	178,157	22,133,858	8,032,293
chn	430,128	104,774,391	25,534,267 a	441,093	115,400,881	28,186,392 a	448,658	128,294,499	32,278,187 a
ccc	21,975	2,489,571	1,194,417	22,349	2,692,651	1,764,264	21,977	3,137,553	1,505,044
cpc	55,577	9,619,526	1,087,680	90,005	11,392,729	1,215,279	88,382	10,919,882	1,648,770
ecc	29,331	3,928,781	896,828	29,636	4,182,648	1,009,726	28,886	4,503,104	1,068,134
ecv	69,960	17,044,074	5,131,124	71,808	19,875,977	6,353,422	73,458	21,451,544	6,898,871
elc	ALC & LCA	ALC & LCA	ALC & LCA	ALC & LCA	ALC & LCA	ALC & LCA	ALC & LCA	ALC & LCA	ALC & LCA
els	13,097	1,519,749	394,725	13,480	1,739,255	573,000	14,504	2,114,998	456,018
emc	3,123	644,548	548,000	NA	NA	NA	3,350	800,000	628,944
feb	NA	NA	NA	NA	NA	NA	NA	NA	NA
fmc	49,314 a	16,734,865	7,373,664	50,632	18,336,422	8,143,838	51,565	19,954,186	9,261,347
fum	NA	NA	NA	56,605	6,428,458	1,551,036	51,032	6,749,045	1,691,190
ggb	NA	NA	NA	NA	NA	NA	NA	NA	NA
lca	2,166,615	228,081,405	44,531,126	2,183,131	222,637,156	55,646,303	2,187,995	243,449,466	58,761,005
lms	2,010,456	249,150,470	55,076,955	2,018,530	266,546,758	55,896,061	2,026,336	287,098,403	56,831,860
mch	92,390	13,792,266	9,887,051	94,209	15,332,908	11,860,385	93,092	17,215,234	12,259,924
mca	25,583	3,304,388	513,685	25,512	3,567,406	552,512	24,938	4,088,195	573,619
nab	41,437	6,604,693	2,142,148	42,122	7,781,298	2,470,317	42,277	8,902,540	3,302,348
opc	NA	NA	NA	NA	NA	NA	10,372	3,287,612	892,889
pch	3,619,768	502,237,350	100,966,089	3,535,825	529,327,006	111,027,318	3,484,985	563,106,353	125,035,379
rca	210,866 a	41,053,364 a	11,470,631 a	212,349 a	44,681,053 a	11,994,379 a	211,628 a	49,083,734 a	13,163,739 a
sda	479,799	67,241,956	166,166,766	495,699	72,060,121	184,689,250	509,792	81,577,130	184,648,454
sbc	12,513,378	1,123,264,849	219,214,770	12,733,124	1,237,594,037	237,452,055	12,917,992	1,382,794,494	262,144,889
ucc	1,841,312	184,292,017	30,243,223	1,818,762	193,524,114	32,125,332	1,801,241	207,486,324	33,862,658
wel	286,858	32,683,492	10,002,869	293,237	35,889,331	11,212,937	297,862	40,017,991	11,300,102
Total	28,144,054	3,113,766,283	790,822,230	28,426,049	3,359,095,603	902,901,429	28,542,929	3,678,586,675	963,445,135

[a]Data obtained from denominational source.

74

Appendix B-1: Church Member Giving, 1968-1994 (continued)

	Data Year 1977			Data Year 1978			Data Year 1979		
	Full/Confirmed Members	Congregational Finances	Benevolences	Full/Confirmed Members	Congregational Finances	Benevolences	Full/Confirmed Members	Congregational Finances	Benevolences
abc	1,146,084 a	172,710,063	27,765,800	1,008,495 a	184,716,172	31,937,862	1,036,054 a	195,986,995	34,992,300
alc	1,772,227	231,960,304	54,085,201	1,773,179	256,371,804	57,145,861	1,768,071	284,019,905	63,903,906
arp	NA	NA	NA	28,644	5,865,416	1,527,561	28,513	6,155,196	1,858,199
bcc	NA	NA	NA	NA	NA	NA	12,923	5,519,037	1,312,046
ccd	817,288	148,880,340	25,698,856	791,633	166,249,455	25,790,367	773,765	172,270,978	27,335,440
oga	171,947	51,969,150	10,001,062	173,753	57,630,848	11,214,530	175,113	65,974,517	12,434,621
cgg	7,595	1,130,000	110,000	7,550	1,135,000	110,000	7,620	1,170,000	105,000
chb	177,534	23,722,817	8,228,903	175,335	25,397,531	9,476,220	172,115	28,422,684	10,161,266
chn	455,100	141,807,024	34,895,751 a	462,124	153,943,138	38,300,431 a	473,726	170,515,940 a	42,087,862 a
ccc	22,171	3,970,337	1,531,645	22,750	4,343,900	1,610,412	23,751	5,054,699	1,849,258
cpc	88,353	11,611,365	1,781,862	88,093	13,657,931	2,136,706	89,218	13,905,745	2,513,625
ecc	28,840	4,860,936	1,132,782	28,712	4,943,032	1,257,777	28,459	5,514,834	1,454,826
ecv	74,060	23,531,176	7,240,548	74,678	26,200,708	8,017,623	76,092	29,987,284	9,400,074
elc	ALC & LCA	ALC & LCA	ALC & LCA	ALC & LCA	ALC & LCA	ALC & LCA	ALC & LCA	ALC & LCA	ALC & LCA
els	14,652	2,290,697	578,390	14,833	2,629,719	839,132	15,081	2,750,703	869,162
emc	NA	NA	NA	3,634	1,281,761	794,896	3,704	1,380,806	828,264
feb	NA	NA	NA	3,956	970,960	745,059	NA	NA	NA
fmc	52,563	22,417,964	10,163,648	55,493	23,911,458	10,121,800	NA	NA	NA
fum	52,599	6,943,990	1,895,984	53,390	8,172,337	1,968,884	51,426	6,662,787	2,131,108
ggb	72,030	9,854,533	747,842	NA	NA	NA	73,046	13,131,345	1,218,763
lca	2,191,942	251,083,883	62,076,894	2,183,666	277,186,563	72,426,148	2,177,231	301,605,382	71,325,097
lms	1,991,408	301,064,630	57,077,162	1,969,279	329,134,237	59,030,753	1,965,422	360,989,735	63,530,596
mch	96,609	18,540,237	12,980,502	97,142	22,922,417	14,070,757	98,027	24,505,346	15,116,762
mca	25,323	4,583,616	581,200	24,854	4,441,750	625,536	24,782	4,600,331	689,070
nab	42,724	10,332,556	3,554,204	42,499	11,629,309	3,559,983	42,779	13,415,024	3,564,339
opc	10,920	3,514,172	931,935	10,939	4,107,705	1,135,388	11,300	4,683,302	1,147,191
pch	3,430,927	633,187,916	130,252,348	3,382,783	692,872,811	128,194,954	3,321,787	776,049,247	148,528,993
rca	210,637 a	53,999,791	14,210,966 a	211,778 a	60,138,720	15,494,816 a	210,700 a	62,997,526 a	16,750,408 a
sda	522,317	98,468,365	216,202,975	535,705	104,044,989	226,692,736	553,089	118,711,906	255,936,372
sbc	13,078,239	1,506,877,921	289,179,711	13,191,394	1,668,120,760	316,462,385	13,372,757	1,864,213,869	355,885,769
ucc	1,785,652	219,878,772	35,522,221	1,769,104	232,593,033	37,789,958	1,745,533	249,443,032	41,100,583
wel	301,944	44,492,259	11,639,834	303,944	50,255,539	12,960,885	306,264	54,983,467	14,230,208
Total	28,641,685	4,003,684,814	1,020,068,226	28,489,339	4,394,869,003	1,091,439,420	28,638,348	4,844,621,622	1,202,261,108

[a] Data obtained from denominational source.

Appendix B-1: Church Member Giving, 1968-1994 (continued)

	Data Year 1980			Data Year 1981			Data Year 1982		
	Full/Confirmed Members	Congregational Finances	Benevolences	Full/Confirmed Members	Congregational Finances	Benevolences	Full/Confirmed Members	Congregational Finances	Benevolences
abc	1,008,700 [a]	213,560,656	37,133,159	989,322 [a]	227,931,461	40,046,261	983,580 [a]	242,750,027	41,457,745
alc	1,763,067	312,592,610	65,235,739	1,758,452	330,155,588	96,102,638	1,758,239	359,848,865	77,010,444
arp	NA	NA	NA	NA	NA	NA	NA	NA	NA
bcc	NA	NA	NA	13,993	6,781,857	1,740,711	NA	NA	NA
ccd	788,394	189,176,399	30,991,519	772,466	211,828,751	31,067,142	770,227	227,178,861	34,307,638
cga	176,429	67,367,485	13,414,112	178,581	78,322,907	14,907,277	184,685	84,896,806	17,171,600
cgg	NA	NA	NA	5,981	1,788,298	403,000	NA	NA	NA
chb	170,839	29,813,265	11,663,976	170,267	31,641,019	12,929,076	168,844	35,064,568	12,844,415
chn	483,101	191,536,556	45,786,446 [a]	490,852	203,145,992	50,084,163 [a]	497,261	221,947,940	53,232,461 [a]
ccc	NA	NA	NA	25,011	8,465,804	2,415,233	26,008	9,230,111	2,574,569
cpc	90,844	16,448,164	2,835,695	91,665	17,225,308	3,504,763	91,774	18,600,022	2,703,521
ecc	27,995	6,043,687	1,517,857	27,567	6,043,687	1,724,722	27,405	6,888,607	1,734,914
ecv	77,737	33,191,322	10,031,072	79,523	37,884,792	8,689,918	81,324	42,599,609	8,830,793
elc	ALC & LCA	ALC & LCA	ALC & LCA	ALC & LCA	ALC & LCA	ALC & LCA	ALC & LCA	ALC & LCA	ALC & LCA
els	14,968	3,154,804	851,308	14,904	3,461,387	716,624	15,165	3,767,977	804,822
emc	3,782	1,527,945	1,041,447	3,753	1,515,975	908,342	3,832	1,985,890	731,510
feb	4,329	1,250,466	627,536	NA	NA	NA	2,047	696,660	1,020,972
fmc	NA	NA	NA	NA	NA	NA	54,198	35,056,434	8,051,593
fum	51,691	9,437,724	2,328,137	51,248	9,551,765	2,449,731	50,601	10,334,180	2,597,215
ggb	74,159	14,967,312	1,547,038	75,028	15,816,060	1,473,070	NA	NA	NA
lca	2,176,991	371,981,816	87,439,137	2,173,558	404,300,509	82,862,299	2,176,265	435,564,519	83,217,264
lms	1,973,958	390,756,268	66,626,364	1,983,198	429,910,406	86,341,102	1,961,260	468,468,156	75,457,846
mch	99,511	28,846,931	16,437,738	99,651	31,304,278	17,448,024	101,501	33,583,338	17,981,274
mca	24,863	5,178,444	860,399	24,500	5,675,495	831,177	24,669	6,049,857	812,015
nab	43,041	12,453,858	3,972,485	43,146	15,513,286	4,420,403	42,735	17,302,952	4,597,515
opc	11,550	5,235,294	1,235,849	11,889	5,939,983	1,382,451	NA	NA	NA
pch	3,262,086	820,218,732	176,172,729	3,202,392	896,641,430	188,576,382	3,157,372	970,223,947	199,331,832
rca	210,762	70,733,297	17,313,239 [a]	210,312	77,044,709	18,193,793 [a]	211,168	82,656,050	19,418,165 [a]
sda	571,141	121,484,768	275,783,385	588,536	133,088,131	297,838,046	606,310	136,877,455	299,437,917
sbc	13,600,126	2,080,375,258	400,976,072	13,782,644	2,336,062,506	443,931,179	13,991,709	2,628,272,553	486,402,607
ucc	1,736,244	278,546,571	44,042,186	1,726,535	300,730,591	48,329,399	1,708,847	323,725,191	52,738,069
wel	308,620	60,624,862	16,037,844	311,351	68,056,396	18,261,099	312,195	71,891,457 [a]	18,677,343
Total	28,754,928	5,336,504,494	1,331,902,468	28,906,325	5,895,828,371	1,477,578,025	29,009,221	6,475,462,032	1,523,146,059

[a] Data obtained from denominational source.

76

Appendix B-1: Church Member Giving, 1968-1994 (continued)

	Data Year 1983			Data Year 1984			Data Year 1985		
	Full/Confirmed Members	Congregational Finances	Benevolences	Full/Confirmed Members	Congregational Finances	Benevolences	Full/Confirmed Members	Congregational Finances	Benevolences
abc	965,117 a	254,716,036	43,683,021	953,945 a	267,556,088	46,232,040	894,732 a	267,694,684	47,201,119 a
alc	1,756,420	375,500,188	84,633,617	1,756,558	413,876,101	86,601,067	1,751,649	428,861,660	87,152,699
arp	31,738	9,695,273 c	3,125,007 d	31,355	11,163,583	2,833,349	32,051	11,839,577	3,360,285
bcc	14,782	7,638,413	1,858,632	15,128	8,160,359	2,586,843	15,535 a	8,504,354 a	2,979,046 a
ccd	761,629	241,934,972	35,809,331	755,233	263,694,210	38,402,791	743,486	274,072,301	40,992,053
oga	182,190	81,309,323	13,896,753	185,404	86,611,269	14,347,570	185,593	91,078,512	15,308,954
cgg	5,759	1,981,300	412,000	4,711	2,211,800	504,200	4,575	2,428,730	582,411
chb	164,680	39,726,743	14,488,192	161,824	37,743,527	15,136,600	159,184	40,658,904	16,509,718
chn	506,439	237,220,642	57,267,073 a	514,937	253,566,280	60,909,810 a	520,741	267,134,078	65,627,515 a
ccc	26,765	9,197,521	2,980,636	28,383	10,018,982	3,051,425	28,624	11,729,365	3,350,021
cpc	93,387	20,206,646	2,604,569	92,242	21,185,481	3,843,056	85,346 a	21,241,302 a	3,227,932 a
ecc	27,203	7,196,283	1,891,486	26,775	7,380,179	2,019,373	26,016	6,147,413	1,777,172
ecv	82,943	46,397,734	10,615,909	84,185	51,613,393	11,243,908	85,150	54,719,309	13,828,030
elc	ALC & LCA	ALC & LCA	ALC & LCA	ALC & LCA	ALC & LCA	ALC & LCA	ALC & LCA	ALC & LCA	ALC & LCA
els	15,576	3,842,625	838,788	15,396	4,647,714	864,714	15,012	4,725,783	791,586
emc	3,857	1,930,689	738,194	3,908	2,017,565	862,350	3,813	2,128,019	1,058,040
feb	2,094	622,467	1,466,399	NA	NA	NA	2,107 a	1,069,851 a	402,611 a
fmc	NA	NA	NA	NA	NA	NA	56,242	42,046,626 a	9,461,369 a
fum	49,441	11,723,240	2,886,931	48,713	11,549,163	2,875,370	48,812	12,601,820	3,012,658
ggb	75,133	17,283,259	1,733,755	75,028	17,599,169	1,729,228	73,040	18,516,252	1,683,130
lca	2,176,772	457,239,780	88,909,363	2,168,594	496,228,216	99,833,067	2,161,216	539,142,069	103,534,375
lms	1,984,199	499,220,552	97,293,050	1,986,392	539,346,935	104,393,798	1,982,753	566,507,516	105,191,123
mch	110,294	34,153,628	17,581,878	90,347	37,333,306	16,944,094	91,167	34,015,200	25,593,500
mca	24,913	6,618,339	911,787	24,269	7,723,611	1,183,741	24,396	8,698,949	1,170,349
nab	43,286	18,010,853	5,132,672	43,215	19,322,720	5,724,552	42,863	20,246,236	5,766,686
opc	12,045	6,874,722	1,755,169	12,239	7,555,006	2,079,924	12,634	8,291,483	2,204,998
pch	3,122,213	1,047,756,995	197,981,080	3,092,151	1,132,098,779	218,412,639	3,057,226 a	1,252,885,684 a	232,487,569 a
rca	211,660	92,071,986	20,632,574 a	209,968 a	100,378,778	21,794,880	209,395	103,428,950	22,233,299
sda	623,563	143,636,140	323,461,439	638,929	155,257,063	319,664,449	651,594	155,077,180	346,251,406
sbc	14,178,051	2,838,573,815	528,781,000	14,341,822	3,094,913,877	567,467,188	14,477,364	3,272,276,486	609,868,694
ucc	1,701,513	332,613,396	55,716,557	1,696,107	385,786,198	58,679,094	1,683,777	409,543,989	62,169,679 a
wel	313,883	76,133,614 a	24,169,441	315,466	82,884,471 a	22,951,699	316,297	87,194,889 a	22,376,423 a
Total	29,267,545	6,921,027,174	1,643,256,303	29,373,224	7,529,423,823	1,733,172,819	29,442,390	8,024,507,171	1,857,154,450

[a] Data obtained from denominational source.

[d] The amounts for Associate Reformed Presbyterian Congregational Finances and Benevolences appear above in reverse order from that presented in the YACC, based on a comparison with other data years.

Appendix B-1: Church Member Giving, 1968-1994 (continued)

	Data Year 1986			Data Year 1987			Data Year 1988		
	Full/Confirmed Members	Congregational Finances	Benevolences	Full/Confirmed Members	Congregational Finances	Benevolences	Full/Confirmed Members	Congregational Finances	Benevolences
abc	862,582 a	287,020,378 a	49,070,083 a	868,189 a	291,606,418 a	55,613,855	825,102 a	296,569,316 a	55,876,771 a
alc	1,740,439	434,641,736	96,147,129	See ELCA	See ELCA	See ELCA	See ELCA	See ELCA	See ELCA
arp	NA	NA	NA	32,289	12,138,959	5,287,424	31,922	13,590,006	5,130,806
bcc	15,911	10,533,883	2,463,558	16,136	11,203,321	3,139,949	NA	NA	NA
ccd	732,466	288,277,386	42,027,504	718,522	287,464,332	42,728,826	707,985	297,187,996	42,226,128
oga	188,662	91,768,855	16,136,647	198,552	124,376,413	20,261,687	198,842	132,384,232	19,781,941
cgg	NA	NA	NA	4,348	2,437,778	738,818	NA	NA	NA
chb	155,967	43,531,293	17,859,101	154,067	45,201,732	19,342,402	151,169	48,008,657	19,701,942 a
chn	529,192	283,189,977	68,438,998 a	541,878	294,160,356	73,033,568	550,700	309,478,442	74,737,057 a
ccc	28,948	15,646,859	3,961,037	29,429	15,509,349	3,740,688	29,015	13,853,547	4,120,974
cpc	91,556	22,992,625	3,782,282	85,781	22,857,711	3,727,681	85,304	23,366,911 e	3,722,607
ecc	25,625	8,619,708	1,399,871	25,300	8,689,978	2,436,473	24,980	12,115,762	2,742,873
ecv	86,079	57,628,572	14,374,707	86,741	61,049,703	14,636,000	87,750	64,920,459	14,471,178
elc	ALC & LCA	ALC & LCA	ALC & LCA	3,952,663	1,083,293,684	169,685,942	3,931,878	1,150,483,034	169,580,472
els	15,082	4,941,917	1,028,974	15,892	5,298,882	1,082,198	NA	NA	NA
emc	NA	NA	NA	3,841	2,332,216	1,326,711	3,879	2,522,533	1,438,459
feb	NA	NA	NA	NA	NA	NA	NA	NA	NA
fmc	56,243	46,150,881	9,446,120	57,262	47,743,298	9,938,096	57,432	48,788,041	9,952,103
fum	48,143	12,790,909	2,916,870	47,173	13,768,272	3,631,353	48,325	14,127,491	3,719,125
ggb	72,263	19,743,265	1,883,826	73,515	20,850,827	1,789,578	74,086	21,218,051	1,731,299
lca	2,157,701	569,250,519	111,871,174	See ELCA	See ELCA	See ELCA	See ELCA	See ELCA	See ELCA
lms	1,974,798	605,768,688	111,938,197	1,973,347	620,271,274	109,681,025	1,962,674	659,288,332	112,694,841
mch	NA	NA	NA	92,902	43,295,100	25,033,600	92,682	47,771,200	27,043,900
mca	24,260	8,133,127	1,155,350	24,440	9,590,658	1,174,593	23,526	9,221,646	1,210,476
nab	42,084	20,961,799	5,982,391	NA	NA	NA	42,629	24,597,288	6,611,840
opc	NA	NA	NA	13,301	9,884,288	2,425,480	NA	NA	NA
pch	3,007,322	1,318,440,264	249,033,881	2,967,781	1,395,501,073	247,234,439	2,929,608	1,439,655,217	284,989,138
rca	207,993	114,231,429	22,954,596	203,581	114,652,192	24,043,270	200,631	127,409,263	25,496,802 a
sda	666,199	166,692,974	361,316,753	675,702	166,939,355	374,830,065	687,200	178,768,967	395,849,223
sbc	14,613,638	3,481,124,471	635,196,984	14,722,617	3,629,842,643	662,455,177	14,812,844	3,706,652,161	689,366,904
ucc	1,676,105	429,340,239	63,808,091	1,662,568	451,700,210	66,870,922	1,644,787	470,747,740	65,734,348
wel	316,416	92,662,969 a	22,448,920	317,294	97,567,101 a	22,207,123	316,987	101,975,092 a	22,406,238
Total	29,335,674	8,434,084,723	1,916,643,044	29,565,111	8,889,227,123	1,968,096,943	29,521,937	9,214,701,384	2,060,337,445

[a]Data obtained from denominational source.

[e]A YACC prepublication data table listed 23,366,911 for Congregational Finances which, added to Benevolences, equals the published Total of 27,089,518.

Appendix B-1: Church Member Giving, 1968-1994 (continued)

	Data Year 1989			Data Year 1990			Data Year 1991		
	Full/Confirmed Members	Congregational Finances	Benevolences	Full/Confirmed Members	Congregational Finances	Benevolences	Full/Confirmed Members	Congregational Finances	Benevolences
abc	789,730 [a]	305,212,094 [a]	55,951,539	764,890 [a]	315,777,005 [a]	54,740,278	773,838 [a]	318,150,548 [a]	52,330,924 [a]
alc	See ELCA	See ELCA	See ELCA	See ELCA	See ELCA	See ELCA	See ELCA	See ELCA	See ELCA
arp	32,600	15,030,209	5,390,867	32,787	16,666,990	5,317,162	33,494	16,932,998	5,907,013 [a]
bcc	16,842	12,840,038	3,370,306	17,277	13,327,414	3,336,580	17,456	14,491,918	3,294,169 [a]
ccd	690,115	310,043,826	42,015,246	678,750	321,569,909	42,607,007	663,336	331,629,009	43,339,307
cga	199,786	134,918,052	20,215,075	205,884	141,375,027	21,087,504	214,743	146,249,447 [a]	21,801,570 [a]
cgg	4,415	3,367,000	686,000	4,399	3,106,729	690,000	4,375	2,756,651	662,500
chb	149,681	51,921,820	19,737,714 [a]	148,253	54,832,226	18,384,483 [a]	147,954	55,035,355 [a]	19,694,919 [a]
chn	558,664	322,924,598	76,625,913 [a]	563,756 [a]	333,397,255 [a]	77,991,665 [a]	572,153	352,654,251	82,276,097 [a]
ccc	28,413	18,199,823	4,064,111	28,355	16,964,128	4,174,133	28,035	17,760,290	4,304,052
cpc	84,866	25,326,430	4,092,869	91,857	28,364,344	4,355,823	91,650 [a]	29,442,581 [a]	5,972,155 [a]
ecc	24,606	10,328,892	2,676,388	24,437	9,946,582	2,442,778	24,383	10,452,528 [a]	3,075,773 [a]
ecv	89,014	66,585,214	15,206,265	89,735	70,568,800	15,601,475	89,648	74,154,515	16,598,656
elc	3,909,302	1,239,433,257	182,386,940	3,898,478	1,318,884,279	184,174,554	3,890,947	1,375,439,787	186,016,168
els	15,740	6,186,648	1,342,321	16,181	6,527,076	1,193,789	16,004	6,657,338	1,030,445
emc	3,888	2,712,843	1,567,728	4,026	2,991,485	1,800,593	3,958	3,394,563	1,790,115
feb	NA	NA	NA	NA	NA	NA	2,008	1,398,968	500,092
fmc	59,418 [a]	50,114,090 [a]	10,311,535 [a]	58,084	55,229,181	10,118,505	57,794	57,880,464	9,876,739
fum	47,228	16,288,644	4,055,624	45,691	10,036,083	2,511,063	NA	NA	NA
ggb	73,738	23,127,835	1,768,804	74,156	23,127,835	1,737,011	71,119 [a]	22,362,874 [a]	1,408,262 [a]
lca	See ELCA	See ELCA	See ELCA	See ELCA	See ELCA	See ELCA	See ELCA	See ELCA	See ELCA
lms	1,961,114	701,701,168 [a]	118,511,582 [a]	1,954,350	712,235,204	129,229,080	1,952,845	741,823,412	124,932,427
mch	92,517	55,353,313	27,873,241	96,487 [a]	65,709,827	28,397,083	99,431	68,926,324	28,464,199
mca	23,802	10,415,640	1,284,233	23,526	10,105,037	1,337,616	22,887	10,095,337	1,205,335
nab	42,629	28,076,077	3,890,017	44,493	31,103,672	7,700,119	43,187 [a]	27,335,239 [a]	7,792,876 [a]
opc	NA	NA	NA	NA	NA	NA	12,265	11,700,000	2,700,000
pch	2,886,482	1,528,450,805	295,365,032	2,847,437	1,530,341,707	294,990,441	2,805,548	1,636,407,042	311,905,934 [a]
rca	198,832	136,796,188 [a]	29,456,132 [a]	197,154	144,357,953 [a]	27,705,029 [a]	193,531	147,532,382 [a]	26,821,721 [a]
sda	701,781	196,204,538	415,752,350	717,446	195,054,218	433,035,080	733,026	201,411,183	456,242,995
sbc	14,907,826	3,873,300,782	712,738,838	15,038,409	4,146,285,561	718,174,874	15,232,347	4,283,283,059	731,812,766
ucc	1,625,969	496,825,160	72,300,698	1,599,212	527,378,397	71,984,897	1,583,830	543,803,752	73,149,887
wel	317,117	110,575,539 [a]	22,811,571	316,813	116,272,092 [a]	24,088,568	316,929 [a]	121,835,547 [a]	24,276,370 [a]
Total	29,536,115	9,752,260,523	2,151,448,939	29,582,323	10,221,536,016	2,188,907,190	29,698,721	10,630,997,362	2,249,183,466

[a]Data obtained from denominational source.

Appendix B-1: Church Member Giving, 1968-1994 (continued)

	Data Year 1992			Data Year 1993			Data Year 1994		
	Full/Confirmed Members	Congregational Finances	Benevolences	Full/Confirmed Members	Congregational Finances	Benevolences	Full/Confirmed Members	Congregational Finances	Benevolences
abc	730,009 [a]	310,307,040 [a]	52,764,005 [a]	764,657 [a]	346,658,047 [a]	53,562,811	697,379 [a]	337,185,885 [a]	51,553,256 [a]
alc	See ELCA	See ELCA	See ELCA	See ELCA	See ELCA	See ELCA	See ELCA	See ELCA	See ELCA
arp	33,550	16,671,405 [a]	6,988,560 [a]	33,662 [a]	18,268,493 [a]	5,822,845 [a]	33,636	20,897,526	6,727,857
bcc	17,646 [a]	15,981,118 [a]	3,159,717 [a]	17,986	13,786,394	4,515,730 [a]	18,152	14,844,672	5,622,005
ccd	655,652	333,629,412	46,440,333	619,028	328,219,027	44,790,415	605,996	342,352,080	43,165,285
cga	214,743	150,115,497	23,500,213	216,117	158,454,703	23,620,177	221,346 [a]	160,694,760 [a]	26,262,049 [a]
cgg	4,085	2,648,085	509,398	4,239	2,793,000	587,705	3,996	2,934,843	475,799
chb	147,912	57,954,895	21,748,320	146,713	56,818,998	23,278,848	144,282	57,210,682	24,155,595
chn	582,804 [a]	361,555,793 [a]	84,118,580 [a]	589,398	369,896,767	87,416,378 [a]	595,303	387,385,034	89,721,860
ccc	30,387	22,979,946	4,311,234	36,864	23,736,161	5,272,184	37,996	23,758,101 [a]	5,240,805 [a]
cpc	92,240	29,721,914	4,588,604	91,489	29,430,921	4,852,663	90,125	31,732,121	4,864,472
ecc	24,150 [a]	11,180,607 [a]	3,086,730 [a]	23,889	11,397,710	3,259,095	23,504	13,931,409	3,269,986
ecv	90,985 [a]	75,806,590 [a]	16,732,701 [a]	89,511	79,741,500	16,482,315	90,919 [a]	86,043,313 [a]	17,874,955 [a]
elc	3,878,055 [a]	1,399,419,800 [a]	189,605,837 [a]	3,861,418	1,452,000,815	188,393,158	3,849,692	1,502,746,601	187,145,886
els	15,929 [a]	6,944,522 [a]	1,271,058 [a]	15,780	6,759,222 [a]	1,100,660	15,960	7,288,521	1,195,698
emc	4,059	3,834,001	2,299,864	4,130 [a]	4,260,307 [a]	1,406,682 [a]	4,225 [a]	4,597,730 [a]	1,533,157 [a]
feb	1,872 [a]	1,343,225 [a]	397,553 [a]	1,866 [a]	1,294,646 [a]	429,023 [a]	1,898 [a]	1,537,041 [a]	395,719 [a]
fmc	58,220	60,584,079	10,591,064	59,156	62,478,294	10,513,187	59,354 [a]	65,359,325 [a]	10,708,854 [a]
fum	NA	NA	NA	NA	NA	NA	NA	NA	NA
ggb	72,388 [a]	21,561,432 [a]	1,402,330 [a]	73,129 [a]	22,376,970 [a]	1,440,342 [a]	71,140 [a]	19,651,624 [a]	2,052,409 [a]
lca	See ELCA	See ELCA	See ELCA	See ELCA	See ELCA	See ELCA	See ELCA	See ELCA	See ELCA
lms	1,953,248	777,467,488	131,684,905	1,945,077	789,821,559	130,761,788	1,944,905	817,412,113	129,525,358
mch	99,446	68,118,202	28,835,719	95,634		27,973,380	87,911 [a]	64,651,639	24,830,192
mca	22,533	10,150,953	1,208,372	22,223	9,675,502	1,191,131	21,448	9,753,010	1,182,778
nab	43,446	28,375,947	7,327,594	43,045	30,676,902	7,454,087	43,236	32,800,560	7,515,707
opc	12,580 [a]	12,466,266 [a]	3,025,824 [a]	12,924 [a]	13,158,089 [a]	3,039,676 [a]	13,970	14,393,880	3,120,454
pch	2,780,406	1,696,092,968	309,069,530	2,742,192	1,700,918,712	310,375,024	2,698,262	1,800,008,292	307,158,749
rca	190,322 [a]	147,181,320 [a]	28,457,900 [a]	188,551 [a]	159,715,941 [a]	26,009,853 [a]	185,242	153,107,408	27,906,830
sda	748,687	191,362,737	476,902,779	761,703	209,524,570	473,769,831	775,349	229,596,444	503,347,816
sbc	15,358,866	4,462,915,112	751,366,698	15,398,642	4,621,157,751	761,298,249	15,614,060	4,915,453,127 [a]	809,966,842 [a]
ucc	1,555,382	521,190,413	73,906,372	1,530,178	550,847,702	71,046,517	1,501,310	556,540,722	67,269,762
wel	316,183 [a]	127,858,970 [a]	26,426,128 [a]	315,871	137,187,582	24,587,988	315,302	142,851,919	23,998,935
Total	29,735,785	10,925,419,757	2,311,727,922	29,705,072	11,282,441,556	2,314,251,742	29,765,898	11,816,720,382	2,387,789,070

[a]Data obtained from denominational source.
Note: Data in italics indicates a change from the previous edition in the series.

80

Appendix B-2: Church Member Giving for 47 Denominations, 1993-1994

	Data Year 1993			Data Year 1994		
	Full/Confirmed Members	Congregational Finances	Benevolences	Full/Confirmed Members	Congregational Finances	Benevolences
Allegheny Wesleyan Methodist Connection (Original Allegheny Conference)	1,905 [a]	3,289,272 [a]	897,184 [a]	1,905	3,500,213	954,931
Baptist Missionary Association of America	230,747 [a]	46,040,786 [a]	11,370,580 [a]	230,171	50,782,987	10,782,987
Christian and Missionary Alliance	147,367	160,150,177	35,542,467	147,560 [a]	170,376,194 [a]	36,407,346 [a]
Church of the Lutheran Confession	6,385	2,971,349	618,443	6,510	3,222,816	672,173
Churches of God General Conference	32,488	15,902,440	3,186,376	31,862	15,716,667	3,295,868
The Episcopal Church	1,570,444	1,365,626,022 [a]	248,071,529 [a]	1,577,996 [a]	1,444,416,489 [a]	252,242,370 [a]
The Evangelical Church	12,332 [a]	9,223,389 [a]	2,440,732 [a]	12,458	9,037,809	2,383,583
Evangelical Presbyterian Church	52,360	62,478,976	6,896,147 [a]	52,241	59,743,295	8,247,437
Gen Assn of Regular Baptist Churches	154,943	102,568,158 [a]	22,379,964	150,745 [a]	102,462,845 [a]	21,514,320 [a]
International Pentecostal Church of Christ	2,664	2,239,547	793,470 [a]	2,668	2,298,803	1,480,862
The Latvian Evangelical Lutheran Church in America	12,137	2,922,135	422,496	11,322	3,246,474	442,618
Mennonite Church, The General Conference	33,629	14,412,556	7,951,676	35,852 [a]	16,093,551 [a]	8,557,126 [a]
Missionary Church, Inc.	28,408	32,585,246	6,791,846	28,821	34,679,795 [a]	7,068,428
Primitive Methodist Church in the U.S.A.	5,384	3,593,848	4,673,814	5,216 [a]	4,377,247 [a]	5,619,446 [a]
The Schwenkfelder Church	2,421	885,674	198,689	2,577	898,946	183,974
United Brethren in Christ	24,616	17,536,704	2,792,622	24,671	15,422,774	2,986,983
The United Methodist Church	8,646,595	2,583,890,618	719,364,661	8,584,125	2,698,513,430	731,838,348
The Wesleyan Church	107,899	112,711,016	20,433,936 [a]	109,694	118,843,931	23,435,980

[a] Data obtained from denominational source.

Appendix B-3.1:   Church Member Giving for Eleven Denominations, 1921-1952, in Current Dollars

Year	Total Contributions	Members	Per Capita Giving
1921	$281,173,263	17,459,611	$16.10
1922	345,995,802	18,257,426	18.95
1923	415,556,876	18,866,775	22.03
1924	443,187,826	19,245,220	23.03
1925	412,658,363	19,474,863	21.19
1926	368,529,223	17,054,404	21.61
1927	459,527,624	20,266,709	22.67
1928	429,947,883	20,910,584	20.56
1929	445,327,233	20,612,910	21.60
1930	419,697,819	20,796,745	20.18
1931	367,158,877	21,508,745	17.07
1932	309,409,873	21,757,411	14.22
1933	260,366,681	21,792,663	11.95
1934	260,681,472	22,105,624	11.79
1935	267,596,925	22,204,355	12.05
1936	279,835,526	21,746,023	12.87
1937	297,134,313	21,906,456	13.56
1938	307,217,666	22,330,090	13.76
1939	302,300,476	23,084,048	13.10
1940	311,362,429	23,671,660	13.15
1941	336,732,622	23,120,929	14.56
1942	358,419,893	23,556,204	15.22
1943	400,742,492	24,679,784	16.24
1944	461,500,396	25,217,319	18.30
1945	551,404,448	25,898,642	21.29
1946	608,165,179	26,158,559	23.25
1947	684,393,895	27,082,905	25.27
1948	775,360,993	27,036,992	28.68
1949	875,069,944	27,611,824	31.69
1950	934,723,015	28,176,095	33.17
1951	1,033,391,527	28,974,314	35.67
1952	1,121,802,639	29,304,909	38.28

Appendix B-3.2: Church Member Giving for Eleven Denominations, 1953-1967

	Data Year 1953		Data Year 1954		Data Year 1955	
	Total Contributions	Per Capita Total Contributions	Total Contributions	Per Capita Total Contributions	Total Contributions	Per Capita Total Contributions
American Baptist (Northern)	$66,557,447 a	$44.50 b	$65,354,184	$43.17	$67,538,753 d	$44.19
Christian Ch (Disciples of Christ)	$60,065,545 c	$32.50 b	$65,925,164	$34.77	$68,611,162 d	$35.96
Church of the Brethren	$7,458,584	$43.78	$7,812,806	$45.88	$9,130,616	$53.00
The Episcopal Church	$84,209,027	$49.02	$92,079,668	$51.84	$97,541,567 d	$50.94 b
Evangelical Lutheran Church in Am.						
The American Lutheran Church	$30,881,256	$55.24	$34,202,987	$58.83	$40,411,856	$67.03
American Lutheran Church	$30,313,907	$48.70	$33,312,926	$51.64	$37,070,341	$55.29
The Evangelical Lutheran Church	$1,953,163	$55.85	$2,268,200	$50.25	$2,635,469	$69.84
United Evangelical Lutheran Ch.	Not Reported: YACC 1955, p. 264		$2,101,026	$44.51	$2,708,747	$55.76
Lutheran Free Church	Not Reported: YACC 1955, p. 264		Not Reported: YACC 1956, p. 276		Not Reported: YACC 1957, p. 284	
Evan. Lutheran Churches, Assn of						
Lutheran Church in America						
United Lutheran Church	$67,721,548	$45.68	$76,304,344	$50.25	$83,170,787	$53.46
General Council Evang Luth Luth Ch						
General Synod of Evan Luth Luth Ch						
United Syn Evang Luth South						
American Evangelical Luth. Ch	Not Reported: YACC 1955, p. 264		Not Reported: YACC 1956, p. 276		Not Reported: YACC 1957, p. 284	
Augustana Lutheran Church	$18,733,019	$53.98	$22,203,098	$62.14	$22,090,350	$60.12
Finnish Luth. Ch (Suomi Synod)	$744,971	$32.12	$674,554	$29.47	$1,059,682	$43.75
Moravian Ch in Am. No. Prov.	$1,235,534	$53.26	$1,461,658	$59.51	$1,241,008	$49.15
Presbyterian Church (U.S.A.)						
United Presbyterian Ch in U.S.A.						
Presbyterian Ch in the U.S.A.	$141,057,179	$56.49	$158,110,613	$61.47	$180,472,698	$68.09
United Presbyterian Ch in N.A.	$13,204,897	$57.73	$14,797,353	$62.37	$16,019,616	$65.39
Presbyterian Church in the U.S.	$56,001,996	$73.99	$59,222,983	$75.54	$66,033,260	$81.43
Reformed Church in America	$13,671,897	$68.57	$14,740,275	$71.87	$17,459,572	$84.05
Southern Baptist Convention	$278,851,129	$39.84	$305,573,654	$42.17	$334,836,283	$44.54
United Church of Christ						
Congregational Christian	$64,061,866	$49.91	$71,786,834	$54.76	$80,519,810	$60.00
Congregational						
Evangelical and Reformed	$31,025,133	$41.24	$36,261,267	$46.83	$41,363,406	$52.74
Evangelical Synod of N.A./German Reformed Church in the U.S.						
The United Methodist Church						
The Evangelical United Brethren	$36,331,994	$50.21	$36,609,598	$50.43	$41,199,631	$56.01
The Methodist Church	$314,521,214	$34.37	$345,416,448	$37.53	$389,490,613	$41.82
Methodist Episcopal Church						
Methodist Episcopal Ch South						
Methodist Protestant Church						
Total	$1,318,601,306		$1,446,219,640		$1,600,655,226	

a In data year 1953, $805,135 has been subtracted from the 1955 Yearbook of American Churches (Edition for 1956) entry. See 1956 Yearbook of American Church for 1957], p. 276, n.1.

b To obtain comparable membership figures in order to calculate giving as a percentage of income based on the revised Total Contributions data, the Total Contributions figure as published in the Yearbook was divided by the published per capita figure yielding a membership figure. The revised Total Contributions figure was then divided by the total calculated membership to obtain the revised per capita figure included in the above table.

c In data year 1953, $5,508,883 has been added to the 1955 Yearbook of American Churches (Edition for 1957), p. 276, n. 4.

d Total Contributions averaged from available data as follows: The Episcopal Church, 1954 and 1956 data; American Baptist Churches, 1954 and 1957 data; Christian (Disiples of Christ), 1954 and 1956 data.

Appendix B-3.2: Church Member Giving for Eleven Denominations, 1953-1967 (continued)

	Data Year 1956		Data Year 1957		Data Year 1958	
	Total Contributions	Per Capita Total Contributions	Total Contributions	Per Capita Total Contributions	Total Contributions	Per Capita Total Contributions
American Baptist (Northern)	$69,723,321 d	$45.21	$71,907,890	$46.23	$70,405,404	$45.03
Christian Ch (Disciples of Christ)	$71,397,159	$37.14	$73,737,955	$37.94	$79,127,458	$41.17
Church of the Brethren	$10,936,285	$63.15	$11,293,388	$64.43	$12,288,049	$70.03
The Episcopal Church	$103,003,465	$52.79	$111,660,728	$53.48	$120,687,177	$58.33
Evangelical Lutheran Church in Am.						
The American Lutheran Church	$45,316,809	$72.35	$44,518,194	$68.80	$47,216,896	$70.89
American Lutheran Church	$39,096,038	$56.47	$44,212,046	$61.95	$45,366,512	$61.74
The Evangelical Lutheran Church	$2,843,527	$73.57	$2,641,201	$65.46	$3,256,050	$77.38
United Evangelical Lutheran Ch.	$2,652,307	$53.14	$3,379,882	$64.70	$3,519,017	$66.31
Lutheran Free Church	Not Reported: YACC 1958, p. 292		Not Reported: YACC 1959, p. 277		Not Reported: YACC 1960, p. 276	
Evan. Lutheran Churches,Assn of						
Lutheran Church in America						
United Lutheran Church	$93,321,223	$58.46	$100,943,860	$61.89	$110,179,054	$66.45
General Council Evang Luth Ch						
General Synod of Evan Luth Ch						
United Syn Evang Luth South						
American Evangelical Luth. Ch	Not Comparable (YACC 1958, p. 292)		$935,319	$59.45	$1,167,503	$72.98
Augustana Lutheran Church	$24,893,792	$66.15	$28,180,152	$72.09	$29,163,771	$73.17
Finnish Luth. Ch (Suomi Synod)	$1,308,026	$51.56	$1,524,299	$58.11	$1,533,058	$61.94
Moravian Church in Am. No. Prov.	$1,740,961	$67.53	$1,776,703	$67.77	$1,816,281	$68.14
Presbyterian Church (U.S.A.)						
United Presbyterian Ch in U.S.A.					$243,000,572	$78.29
Presbyterian Ch in the U.S.A.	$204,208,085	$75.02	$214,253,598	$77.06		
United Presbyterian Ch in N.A.	$18,424,936	$73.30	$19,117,837	$74.24		
Presbyterian Church in the U.S.	$73,477,555	$88.56	$78,426,424	$92.03	$82,760,291	$95.18
Reformed Church in America	$18,718,008	$88.56	$19,658,604	$91.10	$21,550,017	$98.24
Southern Baptist Convention	$372,136,675	$48.17	$397,540,347	$49.99	$419,619,438	$51.04
United Church of Christ						
Congregational Christian	$89,914,505	$65.18	$90,333,453	$64.87	$97,480,446	$69.55
Congregational						
Evangelical and Reformed	$51,519,531	$64.88	$55,718,141	$69.56	$63,419,468	$78.56
Evangelical Synod of N.A./German						
Reformed Church in the U.S.						
The United Methodist Church						
The Evangelical United Brethren	$44,727,060	$60.57	$45,738,332 d	$61.75	$46,749,605 d	$62.93
The Methodist Church	$413,893,955	$43.82	$462,826,269 d	$48.31	$511,758,582	$52.80
Methodist Episcopal Church						
Methodist Episcopal Ch South						
Methodist Protestant Church						
Total	$1,753,253,223		$1,880,324,622		$2,012,064,649	

d Total Contributions averaged from available data as follows: 1956 American Baptist Churches, 1954 and 1957 data; 1957 and 1958 Evangelical United Brethren, 1956 and 1960 data; 1957 The Methodist Church, 1956 and 1958 data.

Appendix B-3.2: Church member Giving for Eleven Denominations, 1953-1967 (Continued)

	Data Year 1959		Data Year 1960		Data Year 1961	
	Total Contributions	Per Capita Total Contributions	Total Contributions	Per Capita Total Contributions	Total Contributions	Per Capita Total Contributions
American Baptist (Northern)	$74,877,669	$48.52	$73,106,232	$48.06	$104,887,025	$68.96
Christian Ch (Disciples of Christ)	$84,375,152 d	$51.22	$86,834,944	$63.26	$89,730,589	$65.31
Church of the Brethren	$12,143,983	$65.27	$12,644,194	$68.33	$13,653,155	$73.33
The Episcopal Church	$130,279,752	$61.36	$140,625,284	$64.51	$154,458,809	$68.30
Evangelical Lutheran Church in America						
The American Lutheran Church					$113,645,260	$73.28
American Lutheran Church	$50,163,078	$73.52	$51,898,875	$74.49		
The Evangelical Lutheran Church	$49,488,063	$65.56	$51,297,348	$66.85		
United Evangelical Lutheran Church	Not Reported: YACC 1961, p. 273		Not Reported: YACC 1963, p. 273			
Lutheran Free Church	$3,354,270	$61.20	$3,618,418	$63.98	$4,316,925	$73.46
Evangelical Lutheran Churches,Assn of	Not Reported: YACC 1961, p. 273		Not Reported: YACC 1963, p. 273			
Lutheran Church in America						
United Lutheran Church	$114,458,260	$68.29	$119,447,895	$70.86	$128,850,845	$76.18
General Council Evang Luth Ch						
General Synod of Evan Luth Ch						
United Syn Evang Luth South						
American Evangelical Lutheran Ch	$1,033,907	$63.83	$1,371,600	$83.63	$1,209,752	$74.89
Augustana Lutheran Church	$31,279,335	$76.97	$33,478,865	$80.88	$37,863,105	$89.37
Finnish Lutheran Ch (Suomi Synod)	$1,685,342	$68.61	$1,860,481	$76.32	$1,744,550	$70.60
Moravian Church in America, No. Prov.	$2,398,565	$89.28	$2,252,536	$82.95	$2,489,930	$90.84
Presbyterian Church (U.S.A.)						
United Presbyterian Ch in U.S.A.	$259,679,057	$82.30	$270,233,943	$84.31	$285,380,476	$87.90
Presbyterian Ch in the U.S.A.						
United Presbyterian Ch in N.A.						
Presbyterian Church in the U.S.	$88,404,631	$99.42	$91,582,428	$101.44	$96,637,354	$105.33
Reformed Church in America	$22,970,935	$103.23	$23,615,749	$104.53	$25,045,773	$108.80
Southern Baptist Convention	$453,338,720	$53.88	$480,608,972	$55.68	$501,301,714	$50.24
United Church of Christ						
Congregational Christian	$100,938,267	$71.12	$104,862,037	$73.20	$105,871,158	$73.72
Congregational						
Evangelical and Reformed	$65,541,874	$80.92	$62,346,084	$76.58	$65,704,662	$80.33
Evangelical Synod of N.A/German						
Reformed Church in the U.S.						
The United Methodist Church						
The Evangelical United Brethren	$47,760,877 e	$64.10	$48,772,149	$65.28	$50,818,912	$68.12
The Methodist Church	$532,854,842 e	$53.97	$553,951,102	$55.14	$581,504,618	$57.27
Methodist Episcopal Church						
Methodist Episcopal Ch South						
Methodist Protestant Church						
Total	$2,127,026,579		$2,214,409,136		$2,365,114,612	

d The 1961 YACC, pa. 273 indicates that this data is not comparable.
e The Evangelical United Brethren and The Methodist Church data is calculated from available data.

Appendix B-3.2: Church Member Giving for Eleven Denominations, 1953-1967 (Continued)

	Data Year 1962		Data Year 1963		Data Year 1964	
	Total Contributions	Per Capita Total Contributions	Total Contributions	Per Capita Total Contributions	Total Contributions	Per Capita Total Contributions
American Baptist (Northern)	$105,667,332	$68.42	$99,001,651	$68.34	$104,699,557	$69.99
Christian Ch (Disciples of Christ)	$91,889,457	$67.20	$96,607,038	$75.81	$102,102,840	$86.44
Church of the Brethren	$14,594,572	$77.88	$14,574,688	$72.06	$15,221,162	$76.08
The Episcopal Church	$155,971,264	$69.80	$171,125,464	$76.20	$175,374,777	$76.66
Evangelical Lutheran Church in America						
The American Lutheran Church	$114,912,112	$72.47	$136,202,292	$81.11	$143,687,165	$83.83
American Lutheran Church						
The Evangelical Lutheran Church						
United Evangelical Luth. Church						
Lutheran Free Church	$4,765,138	$78.68				
Evangelical Luth. Churches,Assn of						
Lutheran Church in America	$185,166,857	$84.98	$157,423,391	$71.45	$170,012,096	$76.35
United Lutheran Church						
General Council Evang Luth Ch						
General Synod of Evan Luth Ch						
United Syn Evang Luth South						
American Evangelical Luth. Ch						
Augustana Lutheran Church						
Finnish Luth. Ch (Suomi Synod)						
Moravian Church in Am., No. Prov.	$2,512,133	$91.92	$2,472,273	$89.29	$2,868,694	$103.54
Presbyterian Church (U.S.A.)						
United Presbyterian Ch in U.S.A.	$288,496,652	$88.08	$297,582,313	$90.46	$304,833,435	$92.29
Presbyterian Ch in the U.S.A.						
United Presbyterian Ch in N.A.						
Presbyterian Church in the U.S.	$99,262,431	$106.96	$102,625,764	$109.46	$108,269,579	$114.61
Reformed Church in America	$25,579,443	$110.16	$26,918,484	$117.58	$29,174,103	$126.44
Southern Baptist Convention	$540,811,457	$53.06	$556,042,694	$53.49	$591,587,981	$55.80
United Church of Christ	$164,858,968	$72.83	$162,379,019	$73.12	$169,208,042	$75.94
Congregational Christian						
Congregational						
Evangelical and Reformed						
Evangelical Synod of N.A./German Reformed Church in the U.S.						
The United Methodist Church						
The Evangelical United Brethren	$54,567,962	$72.91	$49,921,568	$67.37	$56,552,783	$76.34
The Methodist Church	$599,081,561	$58.53	$613,547,721	$59.60	$608,841,881	$59.09
Methodist Episcopal Church						
Methodist Episcopal Ch South						
Methodist Protestant Church						
Total	$2,448,137,339		$2,486,424,360		$2,582,434,095	

NOTE: Data for the years 1965 through 1967 was not available in a form that could be readily analyzed for the present purposes, and therefore data for 1965-1967 was estimated as described in the introductory comments to Appendix B. See Appendix B-1 for 1968-1991 data except for The Episcopal Church and The United Methodist Church, available data for which is presented in the continuation of Appendix B-3 in the table immediately following.

Appendix B-3.3: Church Member Giving for Eleven Denominations, The Episcopal Church and The United Methodist Church, 1968-1994

The Episcopal Church			The United Methodist Church		
Data Year	Total Contributions	Full/Confirmed Membership	Data Year	Total Contributions	Full/Confirmed Membership
1968	Not Reported.	2,259,308	1968	$763,000,434 a	10,849,375 b
1969	$198,728,675	2,238,538	1969	$800,425,000	10,671,774
1970	$248,702,969	2,208,773	1970	$819,945,000	10,509,198
1971	$257,523,469	2,143,557	1971	$843,103,000	10,334,521
1972	$270,245,645	2,099,896	1972	$885,708,000	10,192,265
1973	$287,937,285 c	2,084,845 c	1973	$935,723,000	10,063,046
1974	$305,628,925	2,069,793	1974	$1,009,760,804	9,957,710
1975	$352,243,222	2,051,964	1975	$1,081,080,372	9,861,028
1976	$375,942,065	2,021,057	1976	$1,162,828,991	9,785,534
1977	$401,814,395	2,114,638	1977	$1,264,191,548	9,731,779
1978	$430,116,564	1,975,234	1978	$1,364,460,266	9,653,711
1979	$484,211,412	1,962,062	1979	$1,483,481,986	9,584,771
1980	$507,315,457	1,933,487	1980	$1,632,204,336	9,519,407
1981	$697,816,298	1,930,690	1981	$1,794,706,741	9,457,012
1982	$778,184,068	1,922,205	1982	$1,931,796,533	9,405,164
1983	$876,844,252	1,906,618	1983	$2,049,437,917	9,291,936
1984	$939,796,743	1,896,056	1984	$2,211,306,198	9,266,853
1985	$1,043,117,983	1,881,250	1985	$2,333,928,274	9,192,172
1986	$1,134,455,479	1,756,120	1986	$2,460,079,431	9,124,575
1987	$1,181,378,441	1,741,036	1987	$2,573,748,234	9,055,145
1988	$1,209,378,098	1,725,581	1988	$2,697,918,285	8,979,139
1989	$1,309,243,747	1,714,122	1989	$2,845,998,177	8,904,824
1990	$1,377,794,610	1,698,240	1990	$2,967,535,538	8,853,455
1991	$1,433,467,803	1,615,505	1991	$3,099,522,282	8,789,101
1992	$1,582,457,015 d	1,614,081 d	1992	$3,202,700,721 d	8,726,951 d
1993	$1,613,697,551	1,570,444	1993	$3,303,255,279	8,646,595
1994	$1,696,658,859 d	1,577,996 d	1994	$3,430,351,778	8,584,125

a The Evangelical United Brethren Data Not Reported: YACC 1970, p. 198-200. This figure is the sum of The Methodist Church in 1968, and the Evangelical United Brethren data for 1967.

b This membership figure is an average of the sum of 1967 membership for The Methodist Church and the Evangelical United Brethren and 1969 data for The United Methodist Church.

c The Episcopal Church did not report financial data in the 1970 YACC (pp. 198-200) or the 1975 YACC (p. 236). The 1975 dollar figure is an average of t1972 and 1974 data for The Episcopal Church.

d Data obtained directly from denominational source.

Appendix B-4: Trends in Giving and Membership

Appendix B-4.1: Membership for Seven Denominations, 1968-1994

Year	American Baptist Churches (Total Memb)	Assemblies of God	Baptist General Conference	Christian and Missionary Alliance	Church of God (Cleveland, TN)	Roman Catholic Church	Salvation Army
1968	1,583,560	610,946	100,000	71,656	243,532	47,468,333	329,515
1969	1,528,019	626,660	101,226	70,573	257,995	47,872,089	331,711
1970	1,472,478	625,027	103,955	71,708	272,276	48,214,729	326,934
1971	1,562,636	645,891	108,474	73,547	287,099	48,390,990	335,684
1972	1,484,393	679,813	111,364	77,991	297,103	48,460,427	358,626
1973	1,502,759	700,071	109,033	77,606	313,332	48,465,438	361,571
1974	1,579,029	751,818	111,093	80,412	328,892	48,701,835	366,471
1975	1,603,033	785,348	115,340	83,628	343,249	48,881,872	384,817
1976	1,593,574	898,711	117,973	83,978	365,124	49,325,752	380,618
1977	1,584,517	939,312	120,222	88,763	377,765	49,836,176	396,238
1978	1,589,610	932,365	131,000	88,903	392,551	49,602,035	414,035
1979	1,600,521	958,418	126,800	96,324	441,385	49,812,178	414,659
1980	1,607,541	1,064,490	133,385	106,050	435,012	50,449,842	417,359
1981	1,621,795	1,103,134	127,662	109,558	456,797	51,207,579	414,999
1982	1,637,099	1,119,686	129,928	112,745	463,992	52,088,774	419,475
1983	1,620,153	1,153,935	131,594	117,501	493,904	52,392,934	428,046
1984	1,559,683	1,189,143	131,162	120,250	505,775	52,286,043	420,971
1985	1,576,483	1,235,403	130,193	123,602	521,061	52,654,908	427,825
1986	1,568,778	1,258,724	132,546	130,116	536,346	52,893,217	432,893
1987	1,561,656	1,275,146	136,688	131,354	551,632	53,496,862	434,002
1988	1,548,573	1,275,148	134,396	133,575	566,917	54,918,949	433,448
1989	1,535,971	1,266,982	135,125	134,336	582,203	57,019,948	445,566
1990	1,527,840	1,298,121	133,742	138,071	620,393	58,568,015	445,991
1991	1,534,078	1,324,800	134,717	141,077	646,201	58,267,424	446,403
1992	1,538,710	1,337,321	134,658	142,346	672,008	59,220,723	450,028
1993	1,516,505	1,340,400	134,814	147,367	700,517	59,858,042	450,312
1994	1,507,934	1,354,337	135,128	147,460	722,541	60,190,605	443,246

Note regarding American Baptist Churches in the U.S.A. Total Membership data: Total Membership is used for the American Baptist Churches in the U.S.A. for analyses that consider membership as a percentage of U.S. population. The ABC denominational ofice is the source for this data in the years 1968 and from 1986 through 1992. The year 1969 is an average of the years 1968 and 1970. The year 1978 Total Membership data figure is a *YACC* adjusted figure.

Appendix C: Income and Deflators

Appendix C presents U.S. Per Capita Disposable Personal Income for 1921 through 1994.
The Implicit Price Deflator for National Income is provided for 1921 through 1994. The series keyed to
1987=100 provided deflators only from 1929 through 1994. Therefore, the 1921 through 1928 data was
converted to constant 1958 dollars using the series keyed to 1958=100, and the constant 1958 dollar values were
then converted to constant 1987 dollars using the series keyed to 1987=100.

SOURCES

Income 1921-1928, and Deflator 1921-1928
Historical Statistics of the United States: Colonial Times to 1970 Bicentennial Edition, Part 1 (Washington,
DC: Bureau of the Census, 1975):
    1921-28 Per Capita Disposable Personal Income: Series F 9, p. 224 (F 6-9).
    1921-28 Implicit Price Index GNP (1958=100): Series F 9, p. 224 (F 6-9).

Income 1929-1958, and Deflator 1929-1958
U.S. Department of Commerce, Bureau of Economic Analysis. *National Income and Product Accounts of the
United States: Volume 1, 1929-58.* Washington, DC: U.S. Government Printing Office, Feb. 1993.
    1929-1958 Per Capita Disposable Personal Income: Table 2.1, pp. 30-31
    1929-1958 Implicit Price Deflator for National Income: Table 7.13, p. 171.

Income 1959-1988, and Deflator 1959-1988
U.S. Department of Commerce, Bureau of Economic Analysis. *National Income and Product Accounts of the
United States: Volume 2, 1959-88.* Washington, DC: U.S. Government Printing Office, Sept. 1992.
    1959-1988 Per Capita Disposable Personal Income: Table 2.1, pp. 330.
    1959-1988 Implicit Price Deflator for National Income: Table 7.13, p. 295.

Income 1989, and Deflator 1989
    1989 Per Capita Disposable Personal Income: U.S. Bureau of Economic Analysis, *Survey of Current Business*, Table 2.1, July 1992, p. 57.
    1989-1992 Implicit Price Deflator for National Income: U.S. Bureau of Economic Analysis, *Survey of Current Business*, Table 7.13, July 1992, p. 102.

Income 1990-1992, and Deflator 1990-1992
    1990-1992 Per Capita Disposable Personal Income: U.S. Bureau of Economic Analysis, *Survey of Current Business*, Table 2.1, July 1994, p. 62.
    1990-1992 Implicit Price Deflator for National Income: U.S. Bureau of Economic Analysis, *Survey of Current Business*, Table 7.13, July 1994, p. 107.

Income 1993, and Deflator 1993
    1993 Per Capita Disposable Personal Income: U.S. Bureau of Economic Analysis, *Survey of Current Business*, Table 2.1, July 1995, p. 12.
    1993 Implicit Price Deflator for National Income: U.S. Bureau of Economic Analysis, *Survey of Current Business*, Table 7.13, July 1995, p. 23.

Income 1994, and Deflator 1994
    1994 Per Capita Disposable Personal Income: U.S. Bureau of Economic Analysis, *Survey of Current Business*, Table 2.1, July 1996, p. 9.
    1994 Implicit Price Deflator for National Income: U.S. Bureau of Economic Analysis, *Survey of Current Business*, Table 7.13, October 1995, p. 22.

Appendix C: Income and Deflators

Appendix C: Per Capita Disposable Personal Income and Deflators, 1916-1994

Year	Current $s Per Capita Disposable Personal Income	Implicit Price Deflator GNP [1958= 100]	Implicit Price Deflator Natl Inc [1987= 100]	Year	Current $s Per Capita Disposable Personal Income	Implicit Price Deflator Natl Inc [1987= 100]
1921	$555	54.5		1960	$1,994	25.4
1922	$548	50.1		1961	$2,048	25.7
1923	$623	51.3		1962	$2,137	26.3
1924	$626	51.2		1963	$2,210	26.6
1925	$630	51.9		1964	$2,369	27.1
1926	$659	51.1		1965	$2,527	27.9
1927	$650	50.0		1966	$2,699	29.1
1928	$643	50.8		1967	$2,861	29.9
1929	$672		12.6	1968	$3,077	31.3
1930	$594		12.0	1969	$3,274	32.9
1931	$507		10.8	1970	$3,521	34.7
1932	$384		9.2	1971	$3,779	36.6
1933	$357		9.0	1972	$4,042	38.4
1934	$407		9.9	1973	$4,521	40.9
1935	$455		10.4	1974	$4,893	44.3
1936	$514		10.3	1975	$5,329	48.6
1937	$547		10.9	1976	$5,796	51.7
1938	$499		10.5	1977	$6,316	55.4
1939	$532		10.5	1978	$7,042	59.9
1940	$568		10.7	1979	$7,787	65.2
1941	$689		11.3	1980	$8,576	71.0
1942	$864		12.0	1981	$9,455	77.5
1943	$973		12.1	1982	$9,989	82.4
1944	$1,053		12.1	1983	$10,642	86.2
1945	$1,068		12.8	1984	$11,673	90.3
1946	$1,126		16.4	1985	$12,339	93.8
1947	$1,173		18.4	1986	$13,010	96.6
1948	$1,285		19.8	1987	$13,545	100.0
1949	$1,261		19.5	1988	$14,477	104.0
1950	$1,369		19.9	1989	$15,307	108.7
1951	$1,479		20.9	1990	$16,205	113.5
1952	$1,530		21.0	1991	$16,766	117.6
1953	$1,601		21.4	1992	$17,636	121.5
1954	$1,608		21.7	1993	$18,153	124.6
1955	$1,693		22.4	1994	$19,253	127.1
1956	$1,776		23.1			
1957	$1,840		23.9			
1958	$1,874		24.3			
1959	$1,958		25.1			